CIRCUS BAGGAGE STOCK

FRONT ENDPAPER: George Simonds, driver for Ringling Bros. Circus around 1910, coming up a slight grade onto the showgrounds, keeps his eight greys well lined up. (Note: All body poles are in a straight line with the wagon pole, indicating all eight horses are exerting their power to move the load.) *Author's Collection.*

BACK ENDPAPER: As Boss Hostler, Red Finn, cracks his whip over the heads of the eight Percherons, they all lean into their collars and thus move the massive center pole wagon into position. The photograph was taken at Milwaukee's Lake Front Showgrounds in 1935. *Author's Collection.*

A TRIBUTE TO THE PERCHERON HORSE

CHARLES PHILIP FOX

PRUETT **P**UBLISHING COMPANY
Boulder, Colorado

First Edition

1 2 3 4 5 6 7 8 9

Printed in the United States of America

Library of Congress Cataloging in Publication Data

Fox, Charles Philip, 1913-
   Circus baggage stock, a tribute to the
Percheron horse.

   Includes index.
   1. Circus—United States—History.
2. Percheron horse. I. Title
GV1803.F58   791.3′09   82-7631
ISBN 0-87108-625-5   AACR2

Contents

To my grandsons
Chadwick Charles McKellar
and
Morgan Fox McKellar

Preface

The Draft Horse Journal

PUBLISHED QUARTERLY

SERVING THE HEAVY HORSE & MULE TRADE SINCE 1964

Telephone — Circulation 319-352-4046 — Editor 319-352-5342
Downtown Lutheran Mutual Bldg., 201 1st S.E., Box 670, Waverly, Ia. 50677

In this book, Chappie Fox does for the Percheron Horse and the men who worked with that breed what the talented cartoonist Bill Mauldin did for the infantryman of World War II in his famous book *Up Front*. The Percherons and the men who were charged with keeping them fit and working were the Willies and Joes, the infantry if you please, of the circus.

They were routinely expected to do the difficult, sometimes the dangerous, and not infrequently the nearly impossible on mud lots and steep grades that can best be described in those same terms—nearly impossible. The logistics of moving these huge shows was not unlike that of a military campaign. The motive was profit, and the schedule was not designed for tourists or faint hearts. You cannot meet the payroll without getting to the next town and setting up on time.

Few headlines, except for the case of the occasional disaster, and scant public praise were expected by this crew. They were not the headliners and they knew it. They did their jobs in relative obscurity, with the odd exception such as Jake Posey, and their highest praise was a soft-spoken (or obscene, but sincere) compliment from one of their own.

But they also knew that without them the headliners would be nobodies, and that without their skills and their grey horses, their circus could not move and would surely die. It was with confidence in themselves and their Percheron horses that they went about the daily business of making it all possible for generations of Americans to enjoy the giant spectacle of the CIRCUS. It did not come into your living room, but it sure enough came to your town and down your street, and it was the Percheron horse and the horsemen who brought it there. With, of course, a small assist from the railroads.

Perhaps the highest kind of praise is the unspoken kind. Where you have a difficult and demanding job to do and everyone has enough confidence in you that it is not considered worthy of comment when it is well done. This is also known as having "the public's confidence" and "being taken for granted." For generations the Percheron Horse was exactly that; it had the public's confidence and was taken for granted. Not only in the circus, but in agriculture and in moving the nation's commerce up and down the streets of our great cities. The Percheron Horse has truly been an empire builder on our shores.

So, as a Percheron breeder and a long-time friend and admirer of Chappie Fox, I am delighted that he has added this wonderful and carefully researched tribute to the equine Willies and Joes of the circus to his notable collection of books about the Circuses of America.

Maury Telleen
Waverly, Iowa
July 15, 1981
Editor, *Draft Horse Journal* and President, Draft Horse & Mule Association of America

Prologue

INCORPORATED UNDER THE LAWS OF THE STATE OF ILLINOIS

FORMERLY PERCHERON SOCIETY OF AMERICA.

A NON-PROFIT ORGANIZATION

Box 141
Fredericktown, Ohio 43019

Circus Baggage Stock—A Tribute to the Percheron Horse, is indeed a tribute. C.P. "Chappie" Fox, master of all accumulated knowledge of the circus, its wagons, performers, the horses and their handlers, has assembled the stories, details, and pictures bringing the circus to life.

The draft horses were important in the history of our country—in the fields, on the roads, in the cities to move freight, and in the circus. They not only moved the show from town to town, loaded and unloaded the trains, they made the circus parade an exciting event.

The draft horses (mainly Percherons) and their work with the circus are brought to life in this book. Over the muddy roads, poor grounds, broken-down bridges, rainstorms, and many undesirable conditions, they were the tireless performers working long hours. When the grounds were set up with everything in its place, the harnesses, wagons, and horses were cleaned up and decorated with beautiful plumes on their bridles. They were now ready to put on the circus parade.

The circus coming to town, either moving on the roads for short distances or on the trains, was the highlight of the year. It was recreation for the people. It took the place of TV, movies, and other forms of entertainment. The circus coming to town with all its grandeur would have been impossible without these magnificent Percheron draft horses.

The men who handled these horses, cared for them, and drove them in large hitches were the "Cream of the Crop." Together with the horses, they overcame unbelievable obstacles to keep the circus show rolling.

This book is detailed in describing the job each man, performer, and draft horse had to do to perfection, to keep the show on schedule. The moving of equipment down dark, almost impossible roads, the dust, the many limited facilities described in these authentic stories, are fascinating. The many talents of horses and men are illustrated and told so well that you can almost see the mud and hear the chains on the harness.

A few hours later, with these same horses, workers, wagons, and performers, you experience the beautiful street parade. Horse plumes, all participants in identical suits, bands in full uniform (some riding horses, some riding on the beautiful bandwagons), you can almost see it and hear the bands playing.

Chappie Fox has done a magnificient job assembling beautiful stories from some of the people who worked with the horses. He has also filled this book with extraordinary pictures of Percheron draft horses at work. It was this abundance of knowledge, stories, and pictures accumulated by Mr. Fox that, under his direction, set up the Circus World Musuem and also put on the Schlitz Circus Parade.

This is a book I would recommend to be read by everyone. The older generation can recall some of their childhood memories of the circus and the parade. The younger generation can acquaint themselves with how hard, diligent, and exacting these people and horses worked, sometimes many hours without food, under adverse conditions, to do their job and to put on the show. What an interesting life!

I have known Chappie Fox for about twenty years and was privileged to drive the introductory wagon for the Schlitz Circus Parade each year with four registered Percheron horses. Through this time I have learned that he has taken great effort to have everything as authentic as possible in all his work and also in the production of this fine book.

Ray H. Bast
President, Percheron Horse Association of America

Acknowledgments

Gathering the photographs and information for this book has been rewarding, not only because of the fine results, but because of generous contributions from various people and institutions. I am particularly indebted to:

Robert and Greg Parkinson, circus historians, who direct the Library at the Circus World Museum in Baraboo, Wisconsin

Gene Baxter, Troy, New York

Jim McRoberts, Topeka, Kansas

Jos. Schlitz Brewing Co., Milwaukee, Wisconsin

Barkin-Herman & Assoc., Milwaukee, Wisconsin

Ringling Bros. and Barnum & Bailey Combined Shows, Inc., Washington, D.C.

Billboard Publications, Nashville, Tennessee

Harold Gorsuch, Franklin, Ohio

Bud Dillner, Orlando, Florida

Joe Brislin, Oak Harbor, Washington

J.C. White, St. Marys, Ohio

Harry Shell, Tampa, Florida

Glen Graves, Orlando, Florida

Jerry Booker, San Mateo, California

John Van Matre, Winter Haven, Florida

And to the many long-string drivers with whom I have corresponded over the years, thank you for a myriad of facts and many anecdotes. These circus long-string drivers are:

Frank Updegrove

Henry "Apples" Welsh

Will Brock

Jake Posey

Irvine Hetherington

Jack McCracken

"Buffalo" Gustin

"Deacon" Blanchfield

E.L. "Spike" Hansen

Ed Binner

Jim Traver

"Spot" Welk

Mike Tschudy

"Pinky" Barnes

Harry Baker

Frank Wiseman

The author thanks Ringling Bros. and Barnum & Bailey Combined Shows, Inc., for permission to reproduce in this book material involving circus names that they own. These names are:

Ringling Bros. and Barnum & Bailey Circus

Barnum & Bailey Greatest Show on Earth

Ringling Bros. World's Greatest Shows

Sells-Floto Circus

Hagenbeck-Wallace Circus

Sparks Circus

John Robinson Circus

Al G. Barnes Circus

Buffalo Bill's Wild West

Forepaugh-Sells Bros. Circus

Barnum & Bailey
Greatest Show on Earth

GENERAL OFFICES and WINTERQUARTERS
BRIDGEPORT, CONN.

Bridgeport, Conn., Dec. 3, 1909.

Mr. William P. Hall,
 Lancaster, Mo.

My dear Mr. Hall:-

Yours received and was indeed glad to hear from you. Will be glad to look at them *horses* as soon as possible, in fact we must have them soon to break for entrees, etc.

Regarding baggage horses, will be pleased to patronize you if you can furnish the quality at the right price. We want heavy boned, short coupled chunks, to weigh not less than 1500 pounds up to 1700 or 1800 pounds, dark grays or dapples. They must be the right pattern and sound.

I wish you would upon receipt of this letter have some photographs taken of a few of the spotted and other entree horses you are assembling, and mail to me at once. I want to see about the class you are collecting.

Regarding show property, when I come to look at the horses will look you over.

Very truly yours,

Otto Ringling

In 1909, when this letter was written, the Ringling brothers owned and operated Barnum & Bailey Circus, as well as their own show. Otto Ringling was writing to William Hall, a dealer in circus horses and equipment. The second paragraph is particularly informative. Mr. Ringling spelled out precisely what kind of drafters he wanted. *Circus World Museum, Baraboo, Wisconsin.*

Introduction

Circus baggage stock, or draft horses, as "towners" would say, ruled supreme for about a seventy-year period—the early 1870s to the late 1930s. No big railroad circus could have stayed on the road without them. They were the unsung heroes of the show world. So unheralded were they that they were rarely mentioned, or illustrated, in program, courier, or poster. There was one exception—the posters that advertised the street parade illustrated the baggage stock, but the emphasis was on the cages, tableaux, and bandwagons. Yet it was these magnificent and beautifully trained horses, mostly Percherons, that got the show on and off the lot, and on and off the railroad cars. If they had not performed, the band would not have played and the performers would not have taken bows.

Most of the photographs used in this book were taken after 1910 for two reasons. First of all, prior to this time, generally speaking, the camera was an expensive novelty, so photos of baggage stock in action were scarce. Secondly, in this period of time, a draft horse was so common in the everyday lives of everybody, people with cameras never thought to photograph these horses at work on the circus lot.

These big horses were recorded profusely on film, however, when people photographed the street parade. They were aiming their *Kodaks* at the handsome wagons, the bands, beautiful girls, and exotic animals. It was difficult not to include an eight-horse team of dappled greys in the photograph. So this phase of the daily routine of the baggage stock was an exception and was recorded on film.

I had the opportunity to observe and photograph the circus during the last fifteen years of the baggage stock era. In these, and subsequent years, I also had an opportunity to converse with and exchange letters with a number of Boss Hostlers and long-string drivers. In this book I have used as many direct quotations from their letters and conversations as possible.

It is presumed that all who read this book and pore over the photographs are vitally interested in the circus, or the draft horse, or perhaps both. Thus, we added the last chapter dealing with the "Schlitz Circus Parade" that was staged in Milwaukee in early July each year from 1963 through 1973. Those readers who love horses will enjoy the photographs of these contemporary, magnificent, prize-winning, purebred horses from all over America. Those readers who love the circus will be pleased with the beautiful views of many of the most handsome circus parade wagons ever built—all from the enormous and unequalled collection of the Circus World Museum in Baraboo, Wisconsin.

Jake Posey, long-string driver for many shows, driver of Barnum & Bailey's 40-horse team, and Boss Hostler wrote, when he was ninety years old, "I think horses are better than trucks on a soft lot, or any lot. Give me horses enough to move a show, two trips to a team, and I will move it faster than it can be moved with trucks." This was wishful thinking on Jake's part. Progress is mighty rough on nostalgia.

The baggage stock, an action-packed aspect of the circus, follows the horse-drawn wagon show, the boat show, the spectacle, the street parade, the menagerie, and the big railroad flatcar circus into the barn of oblivion.

Today, however, with approximately forty circuses on the road, nary a one has a draft horse, but the circus itself as a form of amusement lives on and is destined for an eternal existence.

Charles Philip Fox

The grade Percheron became the standard circus draft horse. Because they were basically on the show to pull baggage wagons, these horses were referred to as "Baggage Stock" by the circusmen. The performing horses were called "Ring Stock" because they performed in the rings in the big tent. *Circus World Museum, Baraboo, Wisconsin.*

CHAPTER 1

The Horses

On the travelling circus they were known as "Baggage Stock." To the "towners," they were "draft" horses. All circuses also had "Ring Stock," or horses that performed in the rings in the big tents—we are not concerned with these horses in this book—only the drafters. In actuality they, too, performed, but not in the ring.

Among all the horses that worked for a living in the horse-drawn era of this country's development, the circus draft horse comes nearest to perfection. The baggage stock had brains and common sense. They moved the show on a daily basis, regardless of the weather. They were handy, gentle, good-looking, and strong. Mostly they were Percherons.

In the final analysis, because of all these qualities, they kept the show even with its billing. This was all-important to any circus, because if the show did not arrive in town on the day and date it was billed for, there would be no tickets to sell. The baggage stock got the job done.

When circus owners began the big push of moving their shows from town to town by railroad in the 1870s, the draft horse type went through a transition. A heavier and more drafty style of horse was required. Railroad shows were bigger in all respects—more wagons and heavier wagons; thus more and bigger draft horses were needed to move the equipment. All these vehicles

had to be unloaded from the flatcars, then hauled to the showgrounds maybe a block away, or perhaps a mile or two away.

Wagons had to be spotted on the lot, the street parade hauled downtown and back; then at night the horses had to haul the wagons back to the railroad yards and load them onto the flatcars. These horses put in a busy day. When the showgrounds were soft, due to mud or sand, a tremendous drag was created on the massive wagons, which required the very best in horse and driver to move the show. Such conditions were all in the day's work.

Overland circuses went through a transition period in the early 1920s. Country roads were being gravelled and generally cared for with graders. Some turnpikes were paved with macadam or concrete. Owners of small, horse-drawn overland circuses quickly switched from horses to Model T and Chevy trucks. Before this transition, these shows moved overnight five, eight, or perhaps twelve miles to the next town. Horses walk at about $3\frac{1}{2}$ miles an hour. This controlled the distance that could be travelled between towns.

In the 1860s, before the advent of the circuses that moved by rail, there were a few enormous aggregations that moved overland. These few shows had plenty of good draft stock. Mostly, however, the "mud shows," as the overland shows were called (the thick, roiling dust became mud very quickly on rainy nights) were small in size. Their wagons, likewise, were lightweight vehicles and required horses probably weighing 900 to 1,300 pounds.

Many of the smaller shows used their performing horses and ponies to pull wagons over the road. After all, they reasoned, this ring stock had to walk the route anyway, so they were broken to harness.

The glory days of the baggage stock that we are concerned with in this book cover the period of time from 1872, when the *P.T. Barnum's Greatest Show On Earth* went on rails, to 1940 when the *Cole Bros. Circus* switched from draft horses to trucks and tractors to move their show to and from the rail yards. Cole kept four train teams, but the rest of the stock was sold at the end of the season. That decision was the end of the line for baggage stock on the big circuses in the capacity of moving the show. Caterpillar tractors and Mack trucks pushed the powerful Percherons right off the circus lot, and in the process one of the most picturesque and visible aspects of circus day lost out to progress.

The Percheron was the breed that the circus Boss Hostlers found to be the best for circus work. It was not until the 1920s and 1930s, when the draft horse population in American cities and on farms tumbled as the motor age quickly developed, that the circuses began to find it difficult to get all the Percherons they needed and had to resort to using some Belgians.

Circus draft horses were generally grade type geldings, rarely mares or purebreds. The Percherons were either grey or black; while the few Belgians were sorrel, chestnut, or roan in color.

Clydesdales were never used, as they were considered too leggy and clumsy afoot. Suffolks were too small. Belgians were inclined to be too heavy, were too slow afoot, and gave up too easily. Shires were just too big and could not step lively enough to keep the heavy loads moving under tough conditions, as did the quick-footed Percherons.

In 1936 Ellis McFarland, Secretary and Treasurer of the Percheron Horse Association of America, wrote, "the type of Percheron draft horse wanted was an animal that was thickset, short backed, deep bodied, heavy boned, well muscled, good going, medium sized with a nice head and neck and plenty of quality." These were the features and qualities that Boss Hostlers needed, wanted, and had in years past. That is why they used grade Percherons. The Boss Hostlers also found in the Percherons animals that were quick-footed and had the stamina to keep a heavy wagon moving once it was rolling. The Percheron was agile, quick, and had strength and endurance. They were clean legged, devoid of feather (long hair on the fetlock joint), docile, of good temperament, light on feet, and had good knee action.

The Percheron as a distinct breed entered into the record books early in the nineteenth century. The horse was French bred, mainly in lower Normandy Province in a district known as *La Perche*, from which the breed got its name. Tracing the history of this splendid animal, Wayne Dinsmore, Secretary of the Horse & Mule Association of America, wrote in 1944, "The Moors of North Africa mounted on Arab and Barb horses overcame Spain in AD 711. The Moors then overran western France until they were defeated at Tours in AD 732." Tours is at the southern edge of the district of *La Perche*.

Alvin H. Sanders, a leading authority on the Percheron, commented, "The real origin of the Percheron is involved in almost total obscurity, but that Arab blood was left behind at the time of this crowning disaster to Oriental Arms in Western Europe no one need doubt. We may find in this a possible explanation of the combined style and substance of the grey and white chargers so numerous in the middle ages—a possible cross of the Eastern blood horse upon a weightier western type."

What the circus Boss Hostler saw in Percherons was their power to do heavy work and hold up under it. When the day's work was over, they seemed to still be fresh looking—not hot and tired.

All circuses lavished great care on their draft stock to keep them fit, as an ailing horse was a liability. As a rule, the life span of a draft horse on a circus was six years.

Costs varied in different periods of time, of course, but in 1901 *Billboard Magazine* said that good drafters on the horse market brought $100 to $140 each. If the horse had unusual action and quality, the price ranged from $125 to $210 per animal. These, of course, were for grade drafters, the kind used by commercial firms and construction companies in great quantities. The circuses had to compete to get the best stock available.

Will Brock drove eight-up for the *Barnum & Bailey Greatest Show On Earth*. In one of his letters he reflected on the Percheron as a circus horse:

> You ask me to say something about the Baggage Horse so we go to the lot and into the horse tents. They were always thronged with visitors forever asking the same questions no matter what the town, "Where were you yesterday? Where do you go tomorrow? Why are the horses mostly grey? Isn't it a hard life?" Every day east, west, north and south always the same questions. The horses are grey because they are Percherons, for they are best adapted to the circus of all breeds.
>
> The baggage horse first of all must "car" well, travel in the stockcar every night and not look as though he had no care or feed for a week when you unload in the morning, with a good portion of the town out to look you over to judge by the looks of the horses what the show was likely to be. The Percheron comes out of the car in the morning looking as well as when he went in. They are naturally solid, smoother turned and well filled and stand hard work under adverse conditions, such as soft lots under scorching sun. Mud so deep you couldn't touch bottom with a church steeple or freezing rain with a moderate breeze, and loaded under these conditions for a long run, say, Grand Island, Nebraska, to Denver, or Spokane to Bellingham, and when you unloaded here they are all greys heads up. They can stand more and they do not show the strenuous work they have been through when other teams of different breeds come out on the street looking like a hat rack. This reminds me of Mark Twain in *Roughing It*. He relates hiring a saddle horse in California. He noticed the horse had several fine points. He hung his hat on one of them and rode off.

In 1898, Frank B. Morrison, a professor of animal husbandry at Cornell in Ithaca, New York, published a book titled *Feeds and Feeding*. The book has since been republished many times, because it is considered so basic and understandable. In the book, Morrison talks about the relationship of size and power of draft horses. He states, "Weight is the most important single factor that determines the amount a draft horse can pull. However, as the weight of draft horses increases, the pull they can exert per 100 pounds live weight decreases somewhat. To perform work most efficiently, horses should have energetic but calm dispositions and they must be well trained and driven skillfully and steadily. A nervous, excitable driver cannot get the utmost from his team. Among horses of the same weight those with a greater heart girth and compact muscular build are able to exert greater pull. Horses must also be in proper flesh to do their best."

The interesting point that Professor Morrison makes, that the horse weighing a ton cannot necessarily pull more than a horse weighing 1,700 pounds, was also discovered early-on by circus Boss Hostlers. Using the lighter weight grade Percherons also meant that more horses could be loaded into a stockcar. The circus men liked the action, spirit, and tractability of the dappled grey.

Boss Hostler for the *Al G. Barnes Sells-Floto Circus* in 1938 was Mike Tschudy. When asked about the average weight of circus baggage stock, he wrote, "Now as to weight. The most of them ran from 1,650#, 1,700#, or 1,800#, and occasionally wheelers going 1,900# or a little better. Have just checked through some of my records, and in 1938 here is some of the stock I had:

Higgins	1,750#	Matt	1,750#
Tom	1,920#	Diller	1,650#
Hank	1,800#	Ace	1,645#
Major	1,840#	Chief	1,625#
John	1,825#	Jack	1,740#
Ned	1,690#	Joe	1,770#
Tiger	1,725#	George	1,800#

This is a fair cross section and will give you an idea as to their weights."

Jake Posey was Boss Hostler on the *Buffalo Bill Show* when it played Europe in the early 1900s. In a letter he explained about circus horse weights: "When I was on the Bill Show in Europe I bought 16 grade Belgians, strawberry roan in color and all weighing 1,900# each or more. They were powerful horses. I used them as two eights. However, when I came back to America I had 8 grade Belgians, same color but they weighed only 1,600# each. They could go all around the horses I had in Europe. The big roans were more powerful but were slower and would let a wagon sink in the mud. The little roans were snappy and quick. They did not give the wagon time to sink."

Teams matched in color was a cardinal rule on any circus. They looked better—gave a classy appearance to the entire show —and two, four-horse hitches of greys could be made into an eight-up for the street parade and be nicely matched, for example.

Because the grade Percheron was the dominant breed, the dapple grey was the dominant color. (Note: Percherons are, generally, either black or grey. Greys are usually foaled black, gradually dappling and turning white as they age.) It was also realized by circus men that the white and dapple grey Percherons reflected the sun's hot rays; while dark-colored horses had a tendency to absorb the heat.

In April 1907 *Variety* magazine carried a story that the *Hagenbeck-Wallace Circus* would use all dapple grey baggage stock. B. E. Wallace, an excellent judge of horseflesh, personally picked the entire lot.

Ringling Bros. Circus started the trend to Percheron greys. To insure sufficient available horses of the size and color they wanted, they had dapple grey Percheron stallions on two or three farms around Baraboo, Wisconsin, their winter quarters, whose services were available at a nominal stud fee to all mares around the countryside.

Spike Hansen, who drove for the *Ringling Circus*, made no bones about his breed preference. Said he, "The Percheron has always been my choice of draft animal, both for appearance and performance; especially the beautiful dapple grey with white mane and tail when young, and turning to pure white as time moved on. I recall as a boy when owners of registered Percheron stallions drove about the Wisconsin countryside in buggies with the stud tied behind. They serviced the fine-grade mares of the farms, insuring a continuing source of power for their machinery, also surplus for sale to the milkmen, drays, and express companies in the cities."

When the Ringlings took control of the *Barnum & Bailey Circus* in 1908, Otto Ringling, who was the general manager, imme-diately had his hostlers switch over to dapple greys.

Long-string driver for *Barnum & Bailey* and later the *Combined Shows*, Will Brock, had the best explanation of the preference for greys in a letter he wrote in 1953:

> There is a good reason for all greys—here at the runs is a group of cages to go to the lot, four-horse loads and no four-horse teams at hand. But, you have five or six six-horse teams standing waiting for their trip and no six-horse loads.
>
> Take two 6s, cut the wheelers off of one, and the body pair out of the other, and you have three four-horse teams, all matched greys. Use the fours and send the cages to the lot and on their return put your 6s together and by noon you will have a lineup of six-horse loads waiting for the six-horse teams.
>
> Having all greys you can take any pair out of any team and put them in any other team. By way of comparison, the Barnum Show had colors—bays, blacks, duns, roans, etc. I had a team of eight bays, one came down sick and the only extra horse I could get was a flea bitten white; so for ten days, morning and night, I went up and down the street with seven bays and one white. For parade I used a bay from a train team. Right at this time Mr. Otto [Ringling] was buying horses. Tom Lynch [Boss Hostler] would place an order for so many blacks and so many bays, but when the stock was delivered on the lot, they were all greys. Lynch had found a man he could not argue with.
>
> Say you put six blacks together in the Spring. Gee, ain't they pretty. Oh, yea? In July out in the corn belt, or in the Kansas wheat belt, the sun had faded them and they have sweat out to near bays. You have anything but blacks. The eight bays I had on the Barnum Show for three years. Some held their color quite well, but the near four-horse body was by July a clear light dun, and the rest of the team was so bleached out they did not match at all. So here is another reason for all greys.

Tom Lynch did not like buckskins for a reason other than color. "I never saw a buckskin that could pull a bird off a nest."

Some shows carried a special team just because its color added flash to the parade. John Robinson had sixteen creams and ten spotted horses. Hagenbeck-Wallace used a team of ten sorrels and another team of twelve blacks with white trappings and plumes. The *Adam Forepaugh Show* put twelve dun-colored horses on its lead bandwagon one year.

"I drove eight dun-colored horses on the steam calliope for *Sells-Floto Circus* one year," said Jim Traver. "While we were out in California one of my horses went lame and another took sick. The show had two horses matched in color and size shipped express from a dealer in Chicago all the way to Sacramento to fill out my team."

By the 1920s and 1930s, the last prominent decades of the baggage stock, the circuses were forced to use other colors. With the motor age taking over, the Boss Hostlers simply could not get the greys. Teams of blacks, bays, chestnuts, and some roans began to show up on the lots.

It was the Boss Hostler's preference whether he wanted the manes on the baggage stock clipped. Jake Posey wrote, "I preferred to roach the manes. Horses with long manes became entangled and matted in a lump unless combed out daily. Small cinders would lodge in the mane, and if not discovered would cause a sore neck. It was easier to keep the horses, I figured, if the manes were roached.

"Some drivers would knot the horses tail when we hit a muddy lot. But when the sun came out all tails were washed to get the splashed mud and grime out."

The number of horses on a circus told a great deal about the size. This list was gleaned from *New York Clippers, Billboards,* and other sources. It is intended only to give some examples over the years. It is impossible to state accurately whether these figures are for baggage stock alone.

Year	Circus	Horses
1826	Quick & Mead	2
1828	Buckley & Wicks	40
1834	The Association's Menagerie	120
1835	Turner's Circus	9
1848	Raymond's Mammoth Menagerie	100
1849	Crane & Co's. Great Oriental Circus	240
1851	Spalding & Rogers North American Circus	50
1869	Yankee Robinson Circus	220
1871	Burr Robbins Great American	210
1871	Howes Great London	320
1873	The Great Eastern	190
1873	Montgomery Queen	200
1879	Batchelor & Doris	103
1879	Wm. Main & Burdick	14
1880	Sells Bros.	300
1882	Barnum & London	300
1883	Great Adam Forepaugh	200
1884	S.H. Barrett & Co.	121
1885	Walter L. Main	7
1885	Ringling Bros.	14
1887	Welch Bros.	1
1889	Ringling Bros.	110
1891	Barnum & Bailey	205
1892	Lemen Bros.	95
1893	John H. Sparks	62
1900	Ringling Bros.	360
1902	Busby Bros.	20
1907	Dode Fisk	64
1907	Mighty Haag	100
1908	Rippel New United Wagon Show	27
1908	Frank A. Robbins	200
1909	Norris & Rowe	41
1910	Rice & Bell	20
1915	Welsh Bros. & Lessig	18
1915	M. L. Clark	125
1922	Ringling Bros. Barnum & Bailey	351
1923	Golden Bros.	68
1928	Sparks	90
1930	Sells-Floto	136
1935	Cole Bros.	200

When the Ringling brothers, who owned the *Barnum & Bailey Circus* and the *Ringling Bros. Circus,* decided to put the two great shows out as one entity in 1919, they called it *Ringling Bros. and Barnum & Bailey Combined Shows—The Greatest Show On Earth.*

About this show in the year of 1919, Jack McCracken wrote,

"They had the largest number of baggage stock I ever heard about —a total of 373 horses. They were:

1	10-horse team
15	8-horse teams
24	6-horse teams
16	4-horse teams
14	2-horse teams
6	saddle horses
1	extra

"Tom Lynch was Boss Hostler. George Law and Jim Doyle were assistants on the squadron, and Tin Horn Haley, Blackie Diller, Big Top Dutch, and Bill Fifield were assistants on the lot."

When *Ringling Bros. and Barnum & Bailey Circus* was playing Chicago in 1922, the *Chicago Herald & Examiner* wrote: "Tom Lynch, Boss Hostler of the Circus, said he had 351 horses, mostly grey Percheron grades. He recently purchased 40 more head to replace tractors and some horses that were getting old. Lynch said he now had: 14 8-horse teams, 26 6-horse teams, 16 4-horse teams, 177 Wagons, 114 Drivers, 4 Assistants, Train teams and others."

Unforeseen perils popped up occasionally to haunt circus owner and Boss Hostler alike. On October 11, 1924, *Billboard Magazine* reported that *Ringling Bros. and Barnum & Bailey Circus* changed its route because of an outbreak of hoof-and-mouth disease in northern Texas:

> The Big Show played Dallas, Sept. 29th and Ft. Worth the next day. It was scheduled to exhibit in Ardmore, Oklahoma City, Shawnee and Ada the first four days of October, but these cities were cancelled because of an order issued by the Oklahoma State Board of Agriculture. Messrs. Charles and John Ringling made a special trip to Texas to personally direct the changes in the itinerary made necessary by the quarantine. The circus replaced the lost Oklahoma dates with four cities in Texas south of the quarantine line, which ran from Texarkana west to Sweetwater. When the circus played Dallas all the stock was carefully examined, but was found to be free of the disease.

In 1926 when the *Walter L. Main Circus* was coming out of Florida, "The horses with the show were dipped at the Government quarantine station at Jacksonville on Oct. 10th. Most of Florida is still infected with cattle tick. A government law requires all horses to be deloused before leaving the State," reported *Billboard*.

On another occasion they reported in 1932, "Texas Tick Inspector explained the new law covering the tick question in a certain 13 counties. A circus can come in and play here but when leaving the counties all horses must be inspected. If ticks are found on any one animal, all horses on the show must be dipped then held eight days and dipped again before being released. The Inspector advised his department is a friend of circus people and does not want them in trouble so suggested they avoid these counties while the problem exists."

The heavy horse type made it to center ring in bareback acts. These Percherons and Belgians, of course, were used only in these acts, and never were they harnessed and used as draft horses when they entertained; at least on the railroad shows. There was one occasion when the dapple greys made it to the center ring in a liberty act. In 1944 Arturo Konyot broke eight beautifully matched Percherons for *Ringling Bros. and Barnum & Bailey*. It was a handsome and novel display.

Illustrated in this chapter is a lithograph distributed by the *Al G. Barnes Circus* to advertise and brag about their "Blue Ribbon Prize Winning Horses." It shows dozens of dapple grey Percherons being paraded around the hippodrome track. These horses constituted the baggage stock. An example of the closest the Percheron baggage stock came to "getting into the act," so to speak, occurred a few years later in the same show.

Harry Shell was a steam and air calliopist who played in circus bands. In conversation, he evidenced a fascinating habit of using a long "A" and accenting it on many words. And now, here is the story in Harry's own words:

> I was in the band on the Barnes Show for five years in the early 1930s. One year, I think it was 1933, they had a beautiful Grand Entry. Here, let's check this program—yes, there it is—"Magnificent Inaugural Pageant, circusdom's perpetual appeal to children of all ages—a magnificent prelude of titanic proportion."
> Well, the band led off this Grand Entry—all eighteen of us were

mounted on the dapple grey baggage stock. Here is the way it worked. The driver's helpers brought the horses over to the back door. Here they were "ā'dorned" with some fancy trappings on their bridles and a spangled robe was thrown over them.

The band rode bareback, and we rode two "ā'breast." We rode the same horse every day all season. I usually played trumpet, but if our bass drummer was sick, or off for some reason, I was put on it, and it was a big dude, 14 inches wide and 30 inches high. We musicians, of course, were all decked out in our fancy band uniforms.

So when the whistle blew we struck up the band, and on our big horses led the Grand Entry around the track. When we went out of the tent the men from the draft stock department were there to take the horses back to the stables.

You ask "ā'bout" how many practice sessions we had with these horses at the beginning of the season—well, we had none "ā'tall." We had one rehearsal, and that was it. Nothing would spook these horses. They were used to racket and commotion of all kinds, so a little music in their ears wouldn't bother them.

Once in a while the Percherons got involved in a publicity stunt on which any circus thrives. On July 22, 1926, the *Chicago Herald & Examiner* reported an interesting contest conducted by the Illinois College of Agriculture and the Horse Association of America. The *Ringling Circus* was in town and the contest was between a six-horse team of Percherons and an elephant. "Old John," a huge male, was picked to represent the pachyderms. He lost. He could only pull 4,000 pounds a few feet on the dynomometer. The Percherons handily won the contest. It was later explained that "Old John's" main strength is in pushing, not pulling.

A horrible freak-of-nature accident befell fifteen Percherons on *Christy Bros. Circus* in 1926 when the show was playing Gadsden, Alabama. It brought the show great publicity—the kind the circus could do without. *Billboard* said:

A terrific thunderstorm struck the showgrounds at 10:30 A.M. as the parade was forming. Lightning struck a pole holding a high-tension electric line at the rear of the big top. One of the high voltage wires burned off and fell to the ground. It fell across the pole of the first bandwagon and instantly electricuted all six horses which were shod, of course, with steel shoes and standing on wet ground.

The #2 Bandwagon was a few feet away and the electrical surge killed those six draft horses also. Electricity charged the wet ground around these wagons and it electricuted three of the six horses hitched to the steam calliope which was spotted 50 feet away from the two bandwagons.

Replacement horses were in need when a show enlarged or retired old drafters. Usually this was done over the winter. *Billboard* reported in October of 1925 that, "T. A. Smith has been in Ohio for the last few weeks in search of draft horses for Ringling Bros. and Barnum & Bailey Circus. He succeeded in getting 29 head, consisting of greys, roans, and sorrels. In the lot were several weighing one ton each. They will be taken to winter quarters of the show at Bridgeport, Connecticut."

The *Robbins Bros. Circus*, that wintered at Granger, Iowa, seemed to favor a horse dealer in St. Paul and, occasionally, when the show was playing Minnesota, would pick up a few head. In 1926 Mose Zimmerman of the firm Barrett & Zimmerman Horse Dealers was on the circus lot and sold show owner Fred Buchanan eight dapple greys and six jet blacks. Again the next year, while the show was in Fairmount, Minnesota, this circus took delivery of twenty head of greys and blacks. Not often did a show purchase draft horses locally or from farmers along the route, unless, because of a special set of circumstances, there was a dire need for horses.

The *Cole Bros. Circus* was the last big railroad show to use draft stock—the season was 1940. Joe Wallace was Boss Hostler of fifty head of stock. He had two eight-ups and the rest were six-ups, all greys except one six-horse team of blacks driven by Red Carroll. Red's team wore Ringling harness, which Cole had picked up after *Cole Bros.* disastrous winter quarter's fire of February 1940.

In the 1940 season, Cole used teams to unload the trains. However, trucks pulled the wagons from the railroad yards to the showgrounds. At the lot, Joe Wallace's teams took over the job of spotting the wagons. In 1941 *Cole Bros.* kept four train teams, and Dutch Warner, a long-string driver, took charge of these eight Percherons.

And so ended one of the most memorable aspects of circus

day. We conclude this look at the horses with comments on lead bars and body poles. Without this important rigging, the baggage stock would have been unable to do its job.

For example, the *Hagenbeck-Wallace Circus* hired Jake Posey as Boss Hostler for the 1914 season. Jake tells about the job in his book, *The Last of the 40 Horse Drivers*, published in 1959.

> I reported for work April 1st and found the horses lousy, poor, and their legs bare from the effects of mud fever. Short nine horses, we had just enough rigging (lead bars and body poles) to hitch. Not one extra pair of lead bars. The harness was washed and oiled and repaired. On opening day under canvas in Peru, Indiana, April 21st, while getting the cookhouse and stable wagons off the lot, I had to cut out two 6-horse teams because of breaking lead bars and traces. Charley Corey, the Manager, came by. When I explained the situation to him he asked me what I wanted. I told him to telegraph Wallace & Smith, in Milwaukee for one dozen pairs of traces and to wire the Bode Wagon Co. in Cincinnati for one dozen pairs of lead bars and body poles.
>
> When I arrived on the lot at Cincinnati the lead bars and body poles were there and in a few days the traces arrived. Ben Wallace came on the show with the horses we were short when starting out the season. After that the show moved on schedule.

The end of each wagon pole (11 feet 6 inches long) was equipped with a gooseneck. Each body pole (12 feet long) had a steel ring on one end and a gooseneck at the other. Thus, all of these body poles could be quickly connected. No body pole was ever used between the leaders, as it served no useful purpose. The lead bars were specially made doubletrees, each equipped with a steel ring to slip over the gooseneck and on top of the body pole.

On the circus, singletrees were never equipped with hooks, always rings. Trace chains had T-bars on the ends. They would be fed through the rings on the singletree, then through the proper ring on the trace chain. Every circus wagon had a set of doubletrees hanging below the pole. They were a permanent fixture and were painted and striped like the undercarriage.

The lead bars, which were the doubletrees used by the body pole teams and leaders in a four-, six-, or eight-horse hitch, were rarely painted, as they were dragging on the ground much of the time. The body poles were seldom painted for the same reason.

Some shows did give this equipment a coat of white lead and oil at the beginning of the season, and its handling was another routine that varied from show to show, season to season.

On the *Sells-Floto Circus*, driver Henry Brown recalled, "When we loaded at night the rigging was all dropped alongside the flat next to the run car. When the wagons were all loaded this equipment was all put on the deck of the flat underneath the wagons and alongside of them. Nothing was loaded in the stockcar. In the morning the lead bars and body poles were laid out at the crossing, and the teams picked it up there."

Over on the *Barnum & Bailey Show*, Tom Lynch used different methods during different seasons. "Some years we put it in the stockcars with the horses. Other seasons as the teams made their last trip to the train, the lead bars and body poles were hung on the wagon they just brought to the runs. In the morning this rigging was taken off any wagon. The team used this set all day until they returned that night. With this method it was hard to keep track of equipment and caused a lot of work moving it around from wagon to wagon. Carrying it in the stockcar was most efficient," Lynch said.

Mike Tschudy, Boss Hostler on the *Al G. Barnes Circus*, explained, "The floors of the stockcars were heavy four-inch planking where the horses stood—that is, under their hooves. This left a trough down the center where the lead bars were placed. The body poles were hung on large hooks at the end of the stockcars."

Frank Updegrove drove for *Ringling Bros. and Barnum & Bailey Circus* in the early 1920s. He explained how this rigging was handled on the lot. "When a driver spotted his last wagon on the lot, he unhooked his team from the wagon and body poles and lead bars, then drove off to the stables. All the rigging was left laying on the ground in front of the wagon. The circus had two men whose sole job was to care for this equipment. They would daily check each wagon. They knew how many horses were assigned to the vehicle; thus knew exactly what body poles and lead bars should be there. It was their task to check all equipment over. If they found a cracked singletree, or body pole, they replaced it. The defective equipment was taken to the carpenter shop wagon. Late in the afternoon, when the teams came out of the horse tops, they would be driven to their assigned wagon. There the drivers would find the body poles and lead bars laid out on the ground in front of the wagon. All the driver had to do was to hook up."

The lead bars took constant punishment and had to be checked regularly—a cracked singletree could give way on a soft lot and render the power of the horse, indeed the entire team, useless. A chain is no stronger than its weakest link. The same is true with an eight-horse team. It is no stronger than its weakest link, and the lead bars were the crux of their strength—thus the need for a man to be constantly checking them and the body poles.

Starting in 1872, the bigger circuses began to move from town to town on their own railroad cars. This action began the move to more hefty wagons and bigger, more drafty horses to pull them. The smaller shows continued to move cross-country by horse power, as seen in this photo from George W. Hall's Circus, moving down a dirt road. 1911. *Circus World Museum, Baraboo, Wisconsin.*

Mud shows they were called. Frequently, the performing horses were broken to harness and used to assist in moving the show, as shown in this photo. *Author's Collection.*

These small wagon shows used very lightweight horses and wagons. Typical is this rig on Albert M. Wetter's 1893 Circus. *Author's Collection*.

Heber Bros. Wagon Show paraded this diminutive bandwagon. (1915) *Author's Collection*.

Cook Tent.

J. H. King ....Proprietor
Newton Bortte ....First Cook
Albert Woodside ....Second Cook
Tra Hahn ⎫
Bill White ⎬ ....Dish Washers
Ed. Silk .... ⎫
Joe Mann ...... ⎬ .... Waiters
Charles Revey ⎭

Drivers and Grooms.

Dick Hosler..Boss Hostler
Charles Linley..Assistant
Charles Lynn...Boss Canvasman
F. Alger...Blacksmith
Geo. Hobson..Harnessmaker
Geo. Foster....................Greaser and charge of Hospital

GROOMS.

Steve Smyth....................................Charge of Ring Stock
James Wilson....................................Charge of Principal
M. M. Morse..Charge of Ponies

Jack Robinson   Geo. Smith

DRIVERS.

Wm. Smith (Rocky)............................1st Band Wagon
Ralf Hawley..2nd Band Wagon
W. H. Beebe.........................Four-horse Passenger Hack
H. Potter.............................Two-horse Passenger Hack
G. Fostello.............................Two-horse Passenger Hack
Mike Smith.............................Two-horse Passenger Hack
Douglass Paul.....................................Telegraph Wagon
Wm. Barkley...........................Leader of Baggage Train
Wm. Runyon..1st Canvas Wagon
Charles Miller.......................... ....2nd Canvas Wagon
Geo. Roberts.................................Stake and Chain Wagon

Geo. Carson.....................................Side Pole Wagon
John Nelson.....................................1st Stringer Wagon
Harry Webster.................................2nd Stringer Wagon
John Cortney...Jack Wagon
Clark Wait...1st Plank Wagon
Hank McQueen...................................2nd Plank Wagon
I. Lynch...Reserved Seat Wagon
John Burns.......................................Quarter Pole Wagon
Lem. Culegan...Wardrobe Wagon
E. Woodruff.......................................1st Property Wagon
Frank Carter.....................................2nd Property Wagon
Hugh Molonie.......................................Chandelier Wagon
Scott Wickett....................... ....Pole Wagon
W. Clark...1st Tableau
John Lipkin..2nd Tableau
Frank Rhoton...Lion Den
Wm. Love..Four-horse Cage
Pete Burns..Four-horse Cage
E. Plummer...................... ....Four-horse Cage
Ed. Paton...Four-horse Cage

Jake Cline   Tonie Lewis   John Ryder
Chet Johnson   F. Barker   Ed. Evens
     Charles Barrett   Frank Myers

F. S. Been.. . . ..Driver of Cook Tent Wagon

Canvas Department.

Wm. E. Rhodes....................................Master of Canvas
Charles Rhodes..... ....Second Boss
James McGillis...................................Reserved Seat Man
Harry St. Clair...Blue Seat Man
Dan Webster....................Ring Maker and Back Door Man
Chas. Mayhew.....................................Ticket Wagon Man
Roscoe Dumfee...................... ....Front Door Man
Chris. Keller......................................Stake and Chain Man
Pete Johnson.................................... ....Watchman

W.B. Reynolds was a typical wagon show. Here are three pages from their 1892 annual route book that lists the various wagon-loads that the baggage stock pulled 2,124 miles as the circus played 119 towns. The summary lists the horses and wagons used. *Rick Faber Collection.*

SUMMARY.

Distance traveled...miles 2,124
Total number of people employed 175
Length of season......................................weeks 23
Number of towns visited.. 119
Number of states traversed 4

STABLES.

Total number of Advance Stock........................... 14
Total number of Passenger Horses....................... 18
Total number of Baggage Horses...... 136
Total number of Ring Horses................................ 16
Total number of Ponies.. 10
One large Elephant and two Camels.

WAGONS.

Number of Cages... 12
Number of Baggage Wagons.............................. 20
Ticket Wagon.. 1
Band Wagons.. 2
Passenger Wagons... 7
Advance Wagons.. 4

Size of Big Top, 120 feet around top, with a 50-foot middle piece.

Size of Menagerie, 70 feet around top, with one 30-foot middle piece.

Size of Side Show, 60 feet, with two 30-foot middle pieces.

Size of Dressing Room, 40 x 70 feet.

Four Horse Tents, six poles.

One Cook Tent.

When the big teams were moving about the lot, the drivers always rode the near wheeler. 1936, Newark, New Jersey. *Circus World Musuem, Baraboo, Wisconsin.*

A truly remarkable photograph and a tribute to the dapple grey Percheron. This group posed for the cameraman probably around 1916 on the Ringling Bros. Circus. This is an unparalleled and exceptional assembly of magnificently trained Percherons. Without these horses, the people of "Yourtown" would never have seen a circus performance. *Circus World Museum, Baraboo, Wisconsin.*

Typical horses used by the Ringling Bros. and Barnum & Bailey Circus in the 1920s and 1930s. The Percherons were quiet, surefooted, and powerful. *Gene Baxter Collection.*

A well-matched ten on Ringling Bros. Circus around 1916. These horses stayed together as a team for the entire season. They were stabled together and loaded in the stockcars together. *Author's Collection*.

In 1925, this 8-up was on Ringling Bros. and Barnum & Bailey Circus. *Frank Updegrove Photo*.

When the big show played Chicago in 1936, the Baggage Stock Department posed for this photo (Soldier Field in background). The second man from the left in the foreground is Red Finn, Boss Hostler. The others are his assistants. Note the horseshoers on the right. *Author's Collection.*

In 1915, Jake Posey, Boss Hostler, on black horse and his assistant, Eddie Evans, on white-faced horse, show off their drafters on the Hagenbeck-Wallace Circus. *Author's Collection.*

The Hagenbeck-Wallace Circus had some solid Percheron horses in 1931. This photo was taken in New Brunswick, New Jersey. *Author's Collection.*

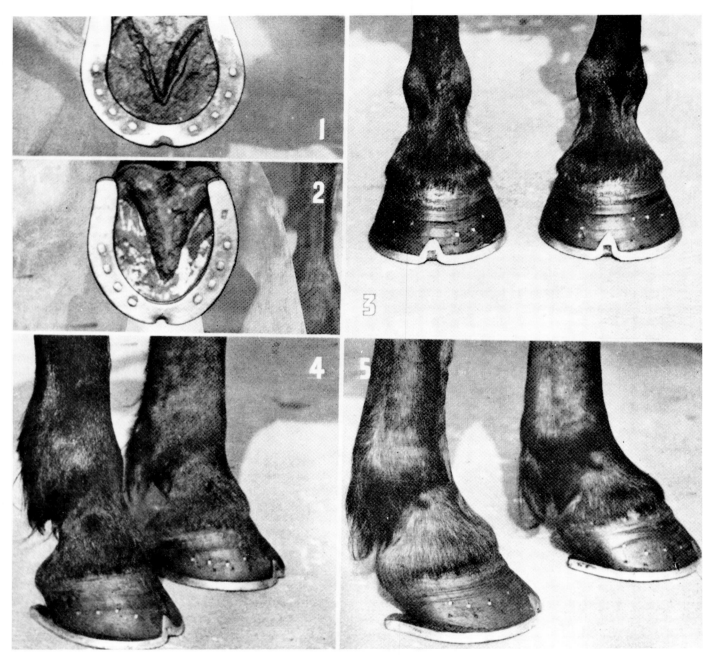

"No foot—no horse," said Ellis McFarland, Secretary-Treasurer of the Percheron Horse Association of America in 1936. "As a breed, the Percheron has the best foot of any of the draft horses." In describing these photos, Mr. McFarland commented, "Picture #3—the best wearing foot usually shows a tough, dense, dark, glistening effect in the outer surface of the hoof wall. Picture #1 is the bottom of the forefoot—large and round. Notice the large V-shaped, well-developed frog, which indicates a healthy foot. Picture #2 shows the bottom of the hindfoot. Notice the broad heel. Picture #4 and #5 are the rear and front feet of a Percheron. Notice the excellent pasterns with good slope and good length." *Percheron Horse Association of America.*

A BIG CONTRACT FOR BIG HORSES

The following article taken from the horse market report of the New York *Herald*, of December 28, 1902, tells its own story:

For the newly equipped Barnum & Bailey shows, which are to open the season at Madison Square Garden about April 1st, Fiss, Doerr & Carroll are now executing the largest contract for high grade draught horses that has ever been filled in the New York market. As heretofore stated in the *Herald*, it calls for three hundred head, and the price to be paid for them is $100,500, or $335 each.

Deliveries on this giant order have lately been begun, and are now progressing at a rate which will complete the contract before March 1st. In company with Joseph D. Carroll, Treasurer and Manager of the Horse Company, James A. Bailey, who is at the head of "the biggest show on earth," personally inspects the animals as fast as they arrive at the Twenty-fourth street stables and accepts those that fill the bill for Barnum & Bailey.

Their facilities for gathering animals of this stamp are not surpassed, if they are equaled, by any other firm in the world.

To meet the terms of the contract every horse must be absolutely sound and from four to seven years old, and he must not be less than sixteen hands nor more than seventeen hands high, and must weigh from sixteen hundred to two thousand pounds, with short legs, deep, full middle, closely ribbed up, sufficient finish and quality, and a good disposition. It is no child's play to find a carload of such horses in the present condition of the draught horse industry, and when it comes to swinging a contract for three hundred head, to be delivered in three months, there are not half a dozen concerns in the whole country that could do it.

In addition to the above three hundred there are over two hundred more horses with the vast exhibition.

Again the following article appeared in the New York *Herald*, of February 8, 1903.

"*Barnum & Bailey buy the Largest Pair of Draught Horses ever seen in this Country.*"

"When the newly equipped Barnum & Bailey shows take the road this season, not the least of their attractions will be the largest pair of draught horses ever sold in the New York market, and probably the largest pair ever worked in this country. After having purchased three hundred fancy draughters from Fiss, Doerr & Carroll, James

INTERIOR OF ONE OF THE BARNUM & BAILEY MAMMOTH HORSE TENTS.

A. Bailey saw this matched pair of equine mammoths and bought them on the spot from Joseph D. Carroll.

The animals stand nearly nineteen hands high, and their size is not misrepresented by their height. Their combined weight, when led on the scales last week, was 4,840 pounds, one of them tipping the beam at 2,480, and the other at 2,360 pounds. There is plenty of bone under them to carry this weight, and big as they are they are built like ponies, with short legs and back, and enormously deep, full middlepieces and broad quarters. Both are bay in color, with white feet and faces.

Fiss, Doerr & Carroll handle thousands of draught horses, but in all their experience they have not found another horse to quite equal either one of these in combined weight, make, quality and manners. Such horses are worth a great deal of money in these days, and Barnum & Bailey paid a fancy price for the pair to use as wheelers in one of their great six-horse teams."

In 1903, the Barnum & Bailey Greatest Show On Earth ran this story in their circus program. *Author's Collection.*

The Breeder's Gazette

VOL. LIX.   CHICAGO, APRIL 19, 1911.   No. 16—1,534.

Horses That Haul the Circus.

HALF OF THE CONSIGNMENT OF DAPPLED GRAY DRAFT HORSES ADDED TO THE CIRCUS STABLES THIS SPRING.

THE public gives little thought to the horses that haul the great circus wagons through the streets. Attention is riveted upon the imposing wagons themselves and the curious animals and luggage with which they are loaded. Yet everyone who views the parade is conscious of a feeling of awe as the magnificent teams and heavy wagons pass by. The draft horses form fully half of the imposing picture presented a curious public. Recollections of the event carry in bold relief the image of numerous and beautiful horses. The horses contribute a potent force toward creating the general impression that the circus is "immense, superb, wonderful, gigantic, ponderous, magnificent, tremendous, extraordinarily splendid, stupendous." Those who are privileged to witness the impressive display of concerted power, when owing to soft ground it may be necessary to put on 20, 30 or 40 big horses to a single wagon, carry away a vivid recollection to intensify their belief in the oft-repeated announcement that the circus is "momentous, incredible, sensational, exciting, marvelous, spectacular, thrilling." For a large collection of high-class draft horses of one stamp and color, impressively hitched and superbly handled nothing excels the big modern circus.

The three great historic circuses now owned by Ringling Bros. are handled when off the railway cars by gray draft horses. The drafters make up a large numerical proportion of the 1,000 horses used altogether in connection with these three shows. It is absolutely necessary to have the wagons furnished with abundant power to take them through any kind of roads and streets and up steep hills. The circus must go at the hour set, no matter what the weather or footing; it brooks no delay, for dates are set far ahead. The wagons are heavy and even the generous number of horses customarily allowed for each is not always enough. The largest wagons weigh as much as 10 to 12 tons with their loads. One time it was necessary to put 40 horses on one of them to take it through a muddy road, and even then it was necessary to stop every couple of rods to shovel out the mud in front of the axles which were buried in the mire. Imagine any other type of horse than drafters pulling together steadily enough for such a job. Each horse has a name and each throws his weight into the collar at the word, and hangs there until the load moves. It is significant of the efficiency of draft horses that they handle satisfactorily this important transportation problem.

Their advertising value is also one of the great assets of the circus equipment. Horses are selected for their striking appearance and attractive beauty of form and color, and they are adorned with handsome brass-mounted harness. The shrewd business calculations of the show managers have settled upon dappled gray as the most impressive color. The stable managers believe that it has been found that as a rule the grays are the best feeders, quiet on the cars and in the stable, quick to learn and easily managed in harness in large teams. They are also declared to be more serviceable than horses of other colors, especially in keeping sound and enduring the summer heat and vicissitudes of travel without sickness. Only geldings are used as they are quieter than mares.

These grays last a long time under this strenuous life. There are six-horse teams that have all worked together for seven or eight years. Many of the horses have never missed a feed in that time and are habitually as round and fat as dumplings. Comparatively low-set wide thick-muscled smooth full-made horses are chosen for this business. Only those horses are accepted that stand upon the greatest and cleanest of bone. Big sound feet are an absolute necessity. The quality chosen is outstanding, and not only must the hair on the legs be as fine as silk but the shorter it is the better.

Reprinted in its entirety is the story, "Horses that Haul the Circus," which appeared in the April 19, 1911 *Breeder's Gazette*, the Bible of the livestock world at the time. *Breeder's Gazette Magazine.*

Every year of late the contract for fresh horses has called for more weight and quality. This year an experiment is being tried with 12 roans as a novelty for the band wagon. These roans and 34 grays were recently delivered to Ringling Bros. by Abe Klee & Son. The consignment made the best and most uniform large lot of big horses seen in Chicago in many months. They were all bought in Illinois, mostly in the central and northern part.

In former years a few horses have been picked from other localities, but when they were put beside the Illinois horses it has been found that they did not measure up to the same high standard. The horses were collected early in the winter and fed in small lots at several points in northern Illinois to put on the requisite finish. For this fattening process they were put into box-stalls so as to allow enough exercise to avoid getting filled hocks, stocked legs and soft muscles. The weights averaged about 1,800 pounds; some weighed as much as 1,925 pounds after shipping to Chicago and none weighed less than 1,600. The contract price is supposed to have been somewhere around $400. Every horse was guaranteed absolutely sound and satisfactory. The average size of the roans and grays was about the same, but the grays were more uniform in quality. When the horses arrived in Chicago an offer of $425 was promptly refused for the roan standing second from the left of the group.

The method of feeding these horses is simple. Results show that it is healthful. Horses are seldom sick. They are habitually given all the timothy hay they want to eat, but with the improvised stables and frequent railway travel the opportunities for quiet eating are not the best. When spring opens and the season's itinerary is begun the horses are put upon a ration of whole oats mixed with bran. This is dampened slightly just before pouring it into the feedboxes. It is dealt out three times a day, giving about all the horses will eat. Bran

mashes are fed as occasion requires. No corn is fed in summer, as it is thought the horses stand the heat, work and heavy feeding better on oats. The summer life is one of hard work, and heavy feeding is necessary to keep up the flesh.

When the circus is loaded upon the railway, the draft horses are put by themselves into long cars. They stand crosswise, crowded closely together without partitions, 24 to 28 in a car. Some of the cars are 50 feet long. Each horse has a D ring in the front of his halter noseband, and into this is snapped a chain about a foot long which is fastened to the side of the car.

When the horses go into winter quarters at the end of the show season the shoes are all pulled off. Each pair of horses stands in a double stall with a 2"x6" plank hung between them to prevent kicking. They are fed corn, preferably on the cob, twice a day, and all the timothy hay they will eat. Each horse is fed separately even in winter and the amount of corn given is regulated by the condition, the object being to put on flesh gradually during cold weather so as to have a reserve to go on during the next summer and to have all the horses as presentable as possible by spring. The horses are turned out during the middle of the winter days for exercise in a lot regulated according to the number of horses. One barn holds 236 horses, another 200; others have less capacity. Each barnful is turned out into a lot just large enough to allow them to move around easily but not to run and fight. The result is that during the whole time they are out a constant milling motion of the herd is maintained. The active horses force the others to move about and all get exercise sufficient to keep them in good condition but not violent enough to afford risk.

A notable feature about the work of circus draft horses is that its intermittent features are even more violent than the alternations of hard and

easy work on the farm, and it necessitates to even a greater extent the frequent hitching of teams together in unusual and large combinations. The fact that big draft horses, combining powerful build with enduring quality, have proved by long experience best adapted to the exacting circus life, indicates that this type of horse should also be best for farm work. In the development of the Ringling Bros.' business from a little traveling company to a combination of three great circuses, the draft horse has been indispensable. He is needed for work, and he does it more economically than any other type of horse. So true is this that there has been a steady increase in the size of horses used. Through mud, rain and heat these horses take their loads. They drink all kinds of water, they work far into the night, they keep irregular hours and spend their rest time largely jostling about in the cars; but their tempers are unruffled, they are always ready for a long hard pull, and always ready for their feed. There is really not a great deal of effort expended upon these horses but they perform an immense amount of heavy tiresome work.

E. T. R.

Hales and Miller, horse dealers in Los Angeles, sold this consignment of 20 drafters to the Al G. Barnes-Sells-Floto Combined Circus in 1938. *Mike Tshudy Collection.*

Over the winter months, Abe Klee and Son advertised in the *Billboard* and the *New York Clipper* that they specialized in circus baggage horses. *Author's Collection.*

Two horse dealers advertised in the January 30, 1904, *New York Clipper*. W.P. Hall was a horse dealer for many years. He also purchased defunct circuses; thus, he got into the selling and leasing of circus equipment, as well as horses. In 1905, he put his own circus on the road. *Author's Collection.*

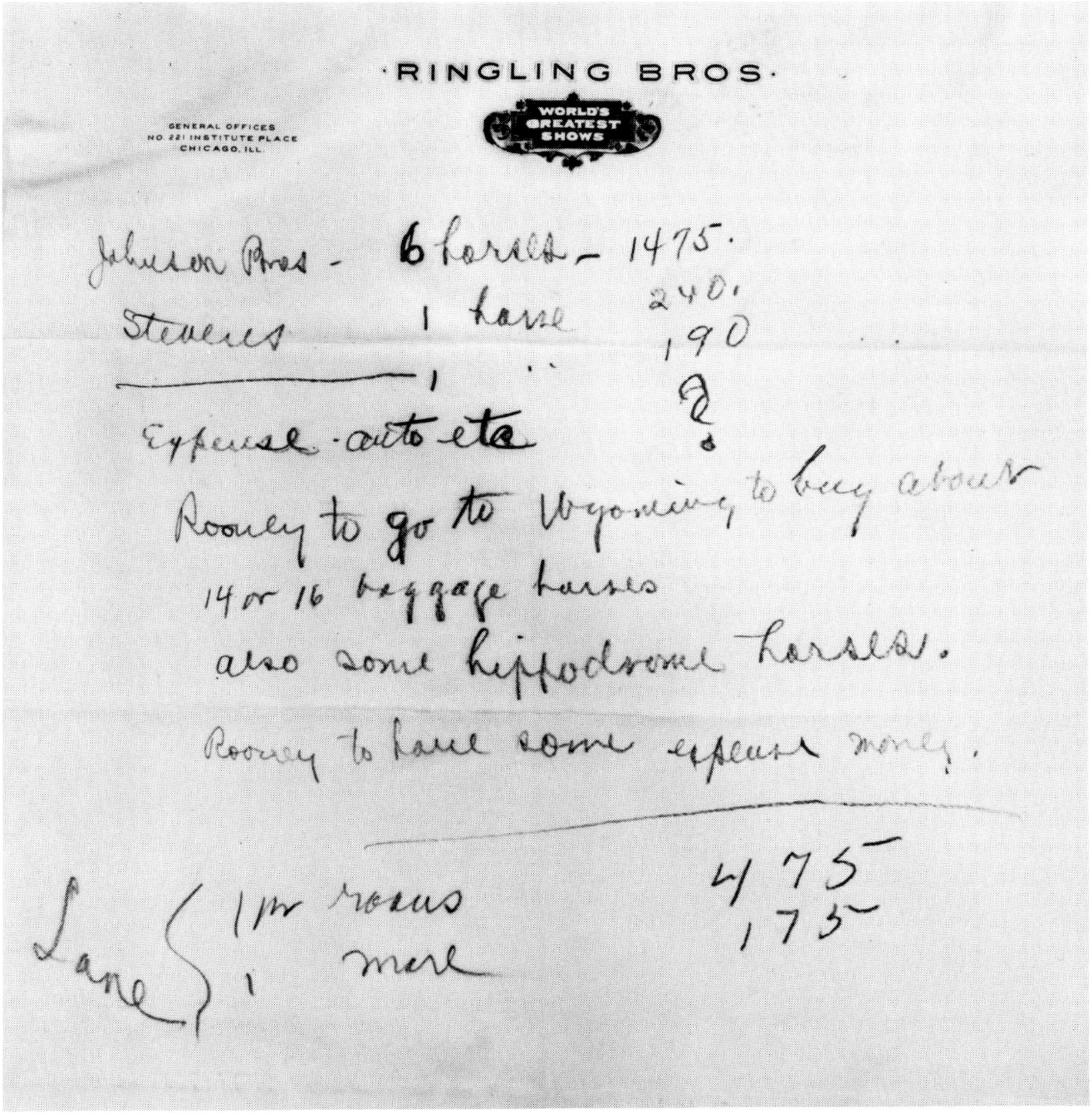

·RINGLING BROS·

GENERAL OFFICES
NO. 221 INSTITUTE PLACE
CHICAGO, ILL.

WORLD'S
GREATEST
SHOWS

Johnson Bros — 6 horses — 1475.
    Stevens   1 horse   240.
    —————— 1   ..   190
Expense · auto · etc   2.

Rooney to go to Wyoming to buy about
14 or 16 baggage horses
also some hippodrome horses.

Rooney to have some expense money.
                                    475
                                    175

Lane { 1 mr roans
       1   mare

The scribbled notations on a letter-head indicate the cost of horses, 1915. Rooney was one of the Hostlers on the show. *Author's Collection.*

A fine, typical team of dapple grey Percherons on Cole Bros. Circus in Fond du Lac, Wisconsin , 1939. These eight horses are well matched in color, size, quality, and temperment. *Author's Photo*.

The near wheel horse. Note the lines neatly looped on the hame. The driver will ride this horse when he moves to his next assignment. *Harold Gorsuch Photo.*

A Cole Bros. wheel team. *Harold Gorsuch Photo.*

Taking it easy while waiting for its next wagon. Ringling Bros. and Barnum & Bailey, 1925. *Frank Updegrove Photo.*

A pair of Ringling wheelers nosing around. These horses work together and are stabled together day in and day out. Note the long neck chains, which means that the horses do not have to carry this equipment. It drags on the ground unless all horses are pulling. 1925. *Frank Updegrove Photo.*

Their eight grade sorrel Belgians strain to take their heavily loaded cookhouse wagon off the lot late in the afternoon. It is Ringling Bros. and Barnum & Bailey Circus in 1937 at Dayton, Ohio. The body poles are all strung out in a straight line with the line pole. The driver's jacket hangs on the hame of the near leader. A few teams of grade Belgians began to appear on the railroad circuses in the 1920s and 1930s because it was so difficult to get the quantity of Percherons needed as the motor age took over and fewer drafters were available. *Harold Gorsuch Photo.*

This 6-up on Cole Bros. Circus has just arrived on the Dayton, Ohio, lot from the runs (1938). This is a good view of the lead horse, body pole, long neck chains, and harness of a typical circus team. *Harold Gorsuch Photo.*

In the late 1920s, the baggage stock kind of backed into recognition on this poster. If there were 350 performing horses, there would have been 390 baggage horses. Not so. Tom Lynch, the Boss Hostler, only claimed 351. The Press Agent came up with the figure used. He realized that the townspeople would never count to see whether there were 740 horses or 540 horses, or even 340 horses, because amid the confusion and excitement of circus day, everybody from eight to eighty would agree that there were hundreds of beautiful horses on the circus. *Author's Collection.*

In 1891, the Percheron was the center of interest on this poster. The artists of the Strobridge Lithograph Company "borrowed" these two magnificent dapple greys from the French artist Rosa Bonheur's famous painting, "The Horse Fair." *Author's Collection.*

AUCTION   AUCTION

Greatest Sale on Record

OF

Circus and Show Property

WILL BE SOLD WITHOUT RESERVE IN SEPARATE LOTS TO THE HIGHEST BIDDER, AT THE WINTER QUARTERS, COLUMBUS, OHIO.

JAN. 10, 11, 12, 1905, COMMENCING AT 10 A. M.

THE

ADAM FOREPAUGH & SELLS BROTHERS' SHOWS.

Consisting in part of 59 R. R. Cars, Sleepers, Box, Stock, Flat and Advertising; 102 Wagons, Tableaux, Band, Chariot, Music and Baggage; 31 Double Cages, carved and gilded, most costly ever made; 16 Trained Elephants, 3 separate performing groups; 26 Camels, 300 valuable Animals—all kinds; 321 Horses, Ring, Menage, Trick, Bareback, Race and Wagon; 19 Ponies, Harness, Trappings and Saddles for 300 Horses. Tents of all sizes, Wardrobe of all kinds—best quality. Portable Seats for 12,000 People, Poles all kinds, Chandeliers, Candy, Side Show and Cooking Outfit, complete; Pictorial Printing, Cuts, Advertising Outfit, Etc., Etc., Etc., Etc., Etc. All can be seen and inspected after DEC. 27, AT COLUMBUS, SALE POSITIVE. NO POSTPONEMENT. NO WITHDRAWALS. Lists on application by mail. Address

ADAM FOREPAUGH & SELLS BROS., 1123 Broadway, N. Y.

Occasionally, the baggage horses were sold at auction when a show folded. This ad in the *New York Clipper*, December 24, 1904, offered the draft stock and wagons along with everything else. James A. Bailey ended up owning this entire circus. *Author's Collection.*

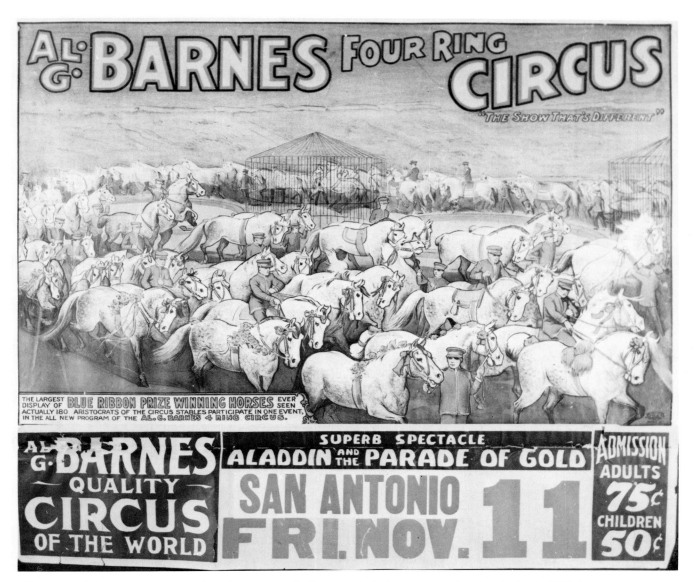

This is one of the rare circus posters that advertised just the baggage stock. In *Billboard Magazine,* April 11, 1925, there was a paragraph stating that Frank Rooney brought 60 head of draft stock around the hippodrome track. Don Francis, who witnessed the spectacular presentation, recalled, "All you could see was horses and dust—I don't know if the dust ever settled." This is as close as the draft horses ever got to being "Center Ring." *Circus World Museum, Baraboo, Wisconsin.*

MR. OGDEN ARMOUR'S CHAMPION TEAM. EXHIBITED ENGLAND, 1907.
NOW BEING TOURED THROUGHOUT THE UNITED STATES WITH THE GREAT SELLS-FLOTO SHOWS.

In 1908, Sells-Floto Circus presented the spectacular International prize-winning Percherons owned by the Armour Packing Company. The circus said that it was the grandest feature ever. All horse lovers would agree. *Author's Collection.*

While waiting for the menagerie tent to be ready for the animal cages, these drafters are resting in the sunshine. The photo was taken October 24, 1924, in Muskogee, Oklahoma. The wagon and the one behind it contain giraffes. The circus was Ringling Bros. and Barnum & Bailey. *Frank Updegrove Photo.*

Typical circus harness. Only the wheelers had breeching. All drivers used hames on which to hang their coats, or rain gear, as can be seen here on the Hagenbeck-Wallace Circus in 1932 at West Allis, Wisconsin. *Author's Photo.*

A Ringling body pole team in 1937. Note the lead bars, body pole, and long neck chains. *Author's Photo*.

Lead bars were frequently carried on wagons in this fashion. Note the use of rings rather than hooks on the singletrees. RBB&B, 1936. *Circus World Museum, Baraboo, Wisconsin*.

Gooseneck end of a body pole with neck chains. Note the steel slipper under the gooseneck. Because these body poles were dragging on the pavement so much of the time, these slippers took the wear. When they became thin, they were replaced. *Author's Photo.*

The ring end of a body pole. The ring slipped over the gooseneck. Body poles were approximately two by three inches and were 12 feet long. *Author's Photo.*

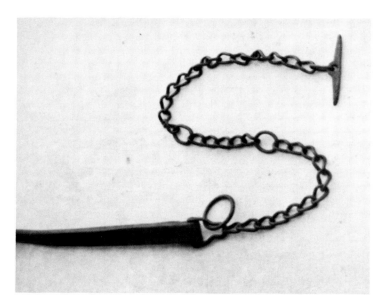

On the end of the trace chains in the 1930s was a six-inch-long "T" bar, as shown. This was threaded through the singletree ring and then through the correct ring on the trace chain. The advantage of this arrangement—it was quick to hook up, and it was failproof. There was no way that it could accidently come apart at a crucial moment. Mud or sand would not interfere with its operation. On occasion, on some shows in some eras, snaps were used on the end of the trace chains. *Author's Collection.*

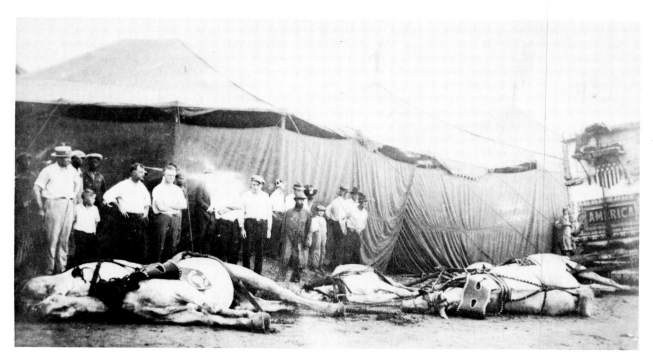

Strange and freak accidents on occasion struck the travelling circus. When Christy Bros. was playing Gadsden, Alabama, in 1926, a violent thunderstorm hit as the show was getting ready to parade. Lightning struck a power pole on the showgrounds, burning off a high-voltage wire and dropping it to the ground. It fell between the wagon and the wheelers, electrocuting all six Percherons as well as a team of six behind this wagon and three horses out of six on a wagon fifty feet away. It was a sickening tragedy for the circus. *Circus World Museum, Baraboo, Wisconsin.*

Ringling bridles in the 1930s were equipped with a snap on the bit. When the horses were loaded into the stockcars, the bit was removed from the horse's mouth and snapped under the chin. *Author's Photo.*

Barnum & Bailey Circus had spent five years in England and Europe. When they returned to the United States, one of the first things that the show did was to order in December 1902 300 Percheron draft horses from a New York horse dealer. Here is a lively engraving used by this dealer on his business envelope. *John Lentz Collection.*

On June 24, 1937, all the drivers on Ringling Bros. and Barnum & Bailey posed for a group photo in Portland, Maine. Red Finn, Boss Hostler, is seated on the left end of the hay bales. With him are two assistants. This was an important group of men to the show. *Author's Collection.*

CHAPTER 2

The Men

The Boss Hostler had one of the most significant and important roles on any show. On his shoulders and those of his assistants rested the responsibility for getting all the wagons from the circus train to the showgrounds, spotting them properly, then hauling the vehicles back to the runs. This chore was accomplished on almost a daily basis, regardless of steep hills enroute to the lot, or mud, or sand at the lot.

The Boss Hostler's department was also in charge of the stables, horseshoeing, hay and grain, veterinarian requirements, and harness repair. His assistants would have various chores allocated to them. Perhaps one in charge of horse tops; one in charge of loading stock into railroad cars; and so forth. In some eras, and on some shows, the Boss Hostler and his crew were also in charge of wagon repair, blacksmithing and greasing of wheels.

The Boss Hostler was an expert on ground conditions. He and his crew could calculate the number of hook rope teams needed, based on the condition of the ground. These men understood sticky red clay, rolling sand, mushy and swampy soil, gooey black gumbo. They understood what these conditions meant to footing for their horses and what the drag would be on the massive wagons.

Boss Hostlers did their work from horseback. They could hustle around the lot; they could see and be seen easily. It was their duty to be on the lot as the teams arrived on the showgrounds and to direct the drivers as to where to spot their wagon. He, of course, could instantly tell the wagon's contents by looking at it or observing its number painted in large letters on front and back of the vehicle (and on some shows on the sides). At night he directed the movements off the lot.

Most all good hostlers knew the names and temperaments of each and every horse in their stables. Frequently, to identify a six- or an eight-horse team, they were referred to by the names of the leaders. A hostler might say to a hook rope team driver, "Go over and give a hand to that Peacock and Eagle team."

The hostlers understood well the importance of never discouraging a team by having a wagon bog down for lack of power. If at all possible, more teams were hooked to a wagon than needed, so that once a wagon started to roll the fast-stepping Percherons could keep it moving. If a wagon sank into mud or sand and came to a stop because of a lack of horse power, it was always tough on horses, men, and equipment to get it rolling again. These hostlers knew their drivers. Tom Lynch, Boss Hostler on *Barnum & Bailey*, 1890 through 1918, then on the *Ringling Bros. and Barnum & Bailey Combined Shows* until he retired in 1934, said, "I can always tell whether a new man was a good driver or not by the way he picked up his lines."

Lynch was a good man. He was a leader, responsible and very resourceful. He kept an eagle eye on his stock, as did his helpers.

They maintained strict discipline—concerned first and always with the horses and their condition. Lynch had very little schooling—he was not much on reading and writing—but when it came to the engineering feat of getting a massive eight-ton loaded wagon out of the mud, he had no peer. Tom Lynch knew every horse under his command by name and in what hitch and what position the horse worked. The most important asset of all was his ability to work his men and get the maximum potential out of them.

In 1906 when he was Boss Hostler on the *Barnum & Bailey Show*, Lynch had these men under him on these jobs: 3 assistants; 1 man in charge of feed; 1 veterinarian; 1 man in charge of lead bars; 2 night watchmen; 3 horseshoers; 2 blacksmiths; 26 eight-horse drivers; 17 six-horse drivers; 22 four-horse drivers; 4 pull-over team drivers; 2 pull-up team drivers; 1 water wagon driver; and 2 harnessmakers. There were a total of 412 draft horses under Tom Lynch's care.

If Lynch faltered on the job, the entire show faltered. His understanding of the massive wagons, knowledge of teaming, comprehension of horses, and his philosophy when working his drivers, got the show to the lot so a performance could be given, so the towners could enjoy the circus. Then, regardless of weather or lot conditions, Lynch got the show back to the runs and loaded on the train, so that people in the next town on the route 100 miles away would be able to enjoy the circus performance, too.

Lynch, or any Boss Hostler, kept the show up with its billing. This is a cardinal rule on any circus of any size—do not ever get behind your billing. Lynch and his Percherons were of paramount importance in getting the show moved. If they failed, if the keystone fell out, there would be a collapse, but this rarely happened on a circus.

Mickey Graves, Property Boss of *Ringling Bros. and Barnum & Bailey Combined Shows*, told the following episode involving Tom Lynch, Boss Hostler. "The season was 1921 and the show was in New England. The lot was tight, very tight. Adjoining the showgrounds was a small church next to which was an ancient cemetery. I was in a discussion with Tom when he broke it off. He saw the horse tent crew starting to drive stakes in the cemetery. Tom bellowed out, 'Hey you sons-of-bitches don't drive stakes there, that's *concentrated* ground.' "

"As to Boss Hostlers I knew, Dave McKay was considered the Dean. We drivers always considered Delavan Alexander the best stable man. Tom Lynch did not have an equal when it came to getting a wagon out of a serious position, hopelessly mired down on a very bad lot. Jake Posey was just a good all-around man with horses. I worked under the last three mentioned," commented Will Brock in a letter. Brock, a *Ringling Bros. and Barnum & Bailey* driver, continued, "The circus is a peculiar business; one the public knows least about. They get out early to watch it unload. They watch it go to the lot. They watch the setup. They watch the tear down. They watch it move off the lot and load up. Then they just wonder how it was done."

Will Brock, who drove an eight-horse hitch, also observed:

It has always seemed a pity to me, the public could not know the sterling quality of these men who moved the show. It required generalship, quick decision, and an ability to get along with all sorts of men and keep them on their toes, fair weather or foul, with scant rest, irregular meals. For instance, in a town where we played only a matinee it was likely we had three meals in three hours; and on a long jump it could happen that you would eat Sunday dinner at 3:00 A.M. on Monday morning. In rainy weather you boarded the sleepers wet through and got out the next morning in a new town with the same wet clothes, with the same rain still pouring down. Men and horses would unload, put the show on the lot, put on the street parade as usual. The horses were always well fed and watered, no matter what the conditions. I know the *Ringling Show* scarcely ever missed a street parade and never in my time got behind their billing, although in case of a blowdown, or storm, they would cancel an evening performance. The work was hard, the hours long, the table fare always the best of everything the market had. Sleeping accommodations were ample. While it really was a hard life, I don't think anyone's days were shortened by working for the circus.

The circus is a peculiar calling in another way in that once settled in the harness, it is a hard thing to get away from. As to our baggage stock, I always felt that the bosses and the drivers loved and admired their horses. The best of hay and grain every day, well watered, washed and groomed daily, harness always ship shape, horses never whipped or flogged—these Percherons moved the show—truly dependable power.

"When it comes to doctoring a sick horse, or a lame one," wrote Jack McCracken, long-string driver, "and when a man has no knowledge of sick animals' care, he is no Boss Hostler. That is a prime requisite for a Boss Hostler."

In the 1930s when Mike Tschudy was Boss Hostler on the *Al G. Barnes-Sells-Floto Combined Shows*, he received a memo each morning from the circus' 24-hour man. "This memo," said Mike, "reached me either at the coaches or the runs, and would advise me of pertinent information such as condition of the lot—whether it was soft, sandy, hard and grassy, or odd shaped. The memo told me how far the lot was; for example, a 3-mile run, or ½-mile run. It would tell me if I had any steep hills to navigate or narrow bridges, or any other worrisome situations. With this information, I could plan for the morning. I would know if I needed extra teams anywhere. It was a good arrangement."

"When I was on the *Al G. Barnes Show*," said Ed Binner, "I remember well our Boss Hostler, Mike Tschudy. He was a good boss and was real concerned with his horses. If he had a sick horse he would doctor it himself. If the show needed more horses he did the buying."

Spencer Alexander was Superintendent of Ringling Bros. baggage stock. Delavan, or Old Del as he was called (he came from Delavan, Wisconsin), was one of the most respected Boss Hostlers in the business. At first he hesitated going with the *Ringling Show*, as he said he could not work for five bosses. Finally he relented and never regretted the move. Delavan explained, "Farmers and livery stable operators along our route got the idea they could bamboozle us and unload all their ailing and decrepit horses on the circus. It never worked, as hostlers had a deep knowledge of horse flesh, and educated fingers run over the animal would quickly reveal any blemishes."

At the beginning of the season each driver was assigned to a team. Depending on his driving ability, he was given an eight-horse team, or perhaps a six or four. Once the Boss Hostler made this decision, the driver had that team for the entire season.

The next step was for the Boss Hostler to assign wagons to various teams. The size and weight of load would determine whether the wagon required an eight-, six-, or four-horse team. Each team was allotted two wagons, generally. In other words, each driver and team would move the same two wagons from the railroad yards to the showgrounds. At night the same teams would pull the same wagons from the lot back to the runs. This meant two trips in the morning and two at night. Of course, when a team brought a wagon onto the lot it also had to spot it in its expected location.

The above mentioned arrangement was generally followed. There were always exceptions to the rule caused by injury to driver, or a horse, or, perhaps, the weather caused changes. Then, too, the process might vary from one circus to another simply because Boss Hostlers had different ideas.

"In my day," Frank Updegrove, eight-horse driver, said, "the Boss Hostler would assign water wagon duty to the drivers. When it was my turn I would take four of my horses and haul the water wagon from fire hydrant to the various departments."

In commenting on drivers, Boss Hostler Jake Posey said, "Strength of arms helps a man in driving a big team, but that isn't the only asset required, a man has to use his head, too. The neatest reinsmen are small and wiry."

Henry Welsh, Boss Hostler on *Forepaugh-Sells Bros. Circus*, remembers Charley Tollworthy as a very fancy driver. "It was the way he held his lines. His leaders had style and action of a pair of coach horses. For a little man he was an exceptional driver."

In a letter Mike Tschudy said, "Blacky Miller was a good all-around man, particularly with eight-up. He was with me about 20 years. Tom O'Brien was the best man who ever worked for me. He was sober, a good driver and caretaker. He drove Gargantua's huge air-conditioned cage around the hippodrome track in 1938."

A good driver had all his horses lined up perfectly and uniformly spaced as to slack, so when he gave them the go-ahead they would all pull evenly without any see-sawing, which caused lost power.

Jake Posey reflected in a letter, "One horse is smarter than the next, and horses have different dispositions. One might be of a mean temperament; the next one gentle; or, perhaps, one likes attention, etc.

"It takes a good driver to understand his horses and get out of a team all there is in it. He must hold his team together, get them to pull together, not one at a time.

"Anyone can get up on a wagon seat behind eight horses, pick up the lines and the team will go down the road. But when you hit a soft lot and there are two or three hook rope teams on your wagon—it is then a driver must know how to do it."

On another occasion Jake Posey explained:

A driver develops extraordinary strength in his fingers, wrists, arms, and back. When a driver climbs up to a wagonseat high over his horses, the first thing he does is to throw the loose ends of the lines behind him on top of the wagon. They are then religiously untangled and laid out flat. The necessity for this is apparent when the team reaches a corner. Let's say he is going to turn left; well, the driver lets the leaders go past the center of the intersection, then while continuing to hold the lines in each hand he makes a quick motion and seizes the lines in his left hand with his right hand and pulls the lines through the left-hand fingers. The near horses get the message and wheel to the left. After the turn, when the team straightens out again, the slack is pulled through the left-hand fingers. If there was a tangle or twist in the lines as they were slipping through his fingers, he is apt to lose the lines when his fingers were forced open.

Going back to the point I made about turning a corner and having the leaders go beyond the center of the intersection—you see if the leaders turned when they hit the intersection then each following team would turn and you would then have the wagon bouncing over the curbs. The driver has to engineer the turn so the wagon stays on the street.

On a downgrade the lines are relatively taut; while on an upgrade they are relatively loose. Here are some additional observations. Wheel horses have to be heavier, smarter, and stronger. It is their duty to keep the wagon on its course. Any Hostler worth his salt aims to bring his stock back to winter quarters at the end of the season in the same condition as when they left in the spring.

Some reporter asked me one day how I knew which line to pull for which horse when I had five lines in each hand. I asked him how does a piano player know which key to strike? He got the message.

Boss Hostlers would forgive most of the sins of long-string drivers, and they had many, except "laying on the leather." Beating a team was never, ever tolerated.

Spot Welk drove an eight on the *Ringling Bros. Circus* in 1907. On the second day of a four-day stand in San Francisco Welk reflected, "The Boss Hostler suddenly realized eight greys were missing from the stable tent. The team's driver, 'Eight-horse Swede' was missing, too. Swede was soon located at the corner saloon, but was unable to give a coherent account. Otto Ringling was by this time furious, and in somewhat of a rage when Swede came to his senses." Welk continued, "Swede was brought to Mr. Ringling and he said, 'Mr. Otto, I needed some beer money so I sold the team.' Well, the team was retrieved the next day and Swede again had the lines. Good long-string drivers with experience were too hard to come by to fire."

"When long string drivers were working," observed Mike Tschudy, "they usually wore rumpled hats, generally felt, or caps. On hot, dusty days they would tie bandanas around their neck. Vests were handy because of the useful pockets. The men never wore gloves and, of course, never carried whips. A whip was a nuisance and also useless. Besides, the men had their hands full of leather anyway. Now, the Boss Hostler and his assistant sometimes carried bullwhips that could be cracked over a lagging horse. That got his attention so he would get moving. The whip was rarely if ever used to hit a horse. The men generally bundled their coats and rain gear and hung them on the hame of one of the horses."

Charley Rooney, a well-respected Boss Hostler on *Ringling Bros.* explained, "Never discourage a team. If I thought an eight on a wagon would have a tough time on a spongy lot, I put on a six as a hook rope team right away before the eight bogged down.

"If a wagon sank into the mud and 36 horses could not move it, I would unhitch all teams and put them on cages or other small wagons they could move with ease. Then I would bring all 36 back to the mired wagon and add another 6 or 8. The wagon moved out. No, don't discourage your horses."

Frank Updegrove, a Pennsylvania farm boy, had an interest in and a love of draft horses. In 1924 he got a job with *Ringling*

Bros. and Barnum & Bailey under Boss Hostler Tom Lynch. His first job was as helper to Dick Sells and his eight-up. One of their assignments was #43 Wagon carrying the center poles for the big top. After three months of learning the ropes, Frank was given a four-horse team of his own. By the end of the season he had a six-up. The next season, 1925, he was given his same six again, but two months later he had graduated to a beautiful team of eight blacks. Frank moved up the ladder fast—it took a natural-born driver to do this.

This is the way these men were broken in during the 1920s and 1930s when there were few drivers with experience driving six or eight or ten horses. Frank Updegrove drove for Ringling during the 1924, 1925, 1926, and 1927 seasons.

Some statistics for 1924 are interesting. The *Big Show* carried approximately 130 wagons most painted red and many with the circus title. The undercarriages were white trimmed in red and blue striping. Two tents were used for the baggage stock, 75-foot round ends with two 60-foot middle pieces or 75-by-195 feet. Eleven stockcars were required to haul the baggage horses—32 horses per car, or a total of 352 head. These were divided into:

> 24 4-horse teams
> 16 6-horse teams
> 18 8-horse teams
> 8 2-horse train teams

In a fascinating letter, E.L. "Spike" Hansen recalls his first year as a baggage stock driver on the *Ringling Show*:

I joined out at the Ringling-Barnum Sarasota winter quarters prior to the 1928 season. Although a "first of May" with the circus, I was no stranger to draft horses, having worked since boyhood on Wisconsin farms, also as a teamster with various firms. Likewise, I loved the circus and the fine horses pulling the wagons in parade. So naturally I sought a job with the baggage stock and Tom Lynch took me on, $5.00 a week and found, assigning me to a six-horse team to clean up and ready for the coming season. The team was Delavan and Jap leaders (they were a good team, but stiff on the bit), Silver and Plato body team, Bob and Baldy wheelers. Jack McCracken once told me they were in the wheel of the eight-horse band team he drove in 1920, hauling the "Two Hemispheres"

wagon, carrying Merle Evans' band, which was the final season for daily parade by the Big One. I believe this was the first year (1928) the Sarasota quarters were used. There were two separate stables for baggage stock, the covered stables forming a square with a spacious open area in the center for exercising, etc. Here the drivers assembled their teams and drove them unattached to wagons for the most part. This was a familiar scene in the old days when returning to either train or lot after delivering a loaded wagon. It was described as "travelling light."

The performing contingent of the show left for the New York Madison Square engagement, opening April 5-28. (I still have that old route card, creased and worn from carrying in my pocket.)

The balance of the show followed later when we left quarters Sunday, April 22, for Washington, D.C. for the first stand under canvas on April 30-May 1.

We were several days enroute, with necessary stops to feed and water. Weather was pleasant through the several southern states and I got out on the flats, sitting atop a wagon to view the scenery. As the train moved slowly through the small town of Jessup, Georgia, several flats became derailed, uncoupling the one on which I was riding. The wagon came unchocked and being at the end of the flat, proceeded to descend onto the rail bed. I made a quick jump from the footboard onto the ground, quite a distance. The train was halted, cars replaced on rails, and the wagon with only the front of it hanging over the flat, pulled back into position and rechocked securely.

When I was hired, of course, it was as a helper, as Tom Lynch had no knowledge of my driving experience, except that I was no show driver. He said he would have plenty of his regular drivers waiting at the runs when the show arrived in D.C. However, when we arrived, there was no one to take over my team, so I put them together and drove on up to the crossing. There was a wagon waiting to be hauled away, so I hooked onto it and proceeded onto the lot. My first experience pulling a circus wagon. The stable tops were not yet erected when I got to the lot; nor was the cook-house flag flying. Anyway, I spotted my wagon where it was directed, glad my "maiden" trip was over.

Several days elapsed, still no driver for the team. Time was nearing for the baggage stock to leave for New York to move the show out of the Garden April 28th. Accordingly, Henry (Apples) Welsh, who was first assistant to Lynch, made the schedule of wagons each team was to handle on closing night. Some teams were split, mine included, leaving me only the body team and wheelers. We loaded Friday afternoon, April 27th, in a freezing rain, mixed with sleet, quite a contrast to the Florida sun we had recently left. We arrived in Jersey City where the train was spotted. We were given meal tickets at a nearby restaurant and bar (I recall its floor was sanded) and awaited the time when we were to ferry across to NYC. My first visit to the Big Apple, and that on horseback, astride a circus baggage horse.

As is often the case, the planned assignment schedule of wagons did not work out; partly due, no doubt, that Kelly Transfer and Drayage Co. were also hired to assist in the hauling. I observed one of their teams, harnessed three abreast, moving one of our wagons at a fast trot. Anyway, I waited for hours on the street outside the Garden until finally I was notified to leave; my load apparently handled by someone else. So I high-tailed it back to the train and loaded my team for the return to Washington.

A driver was finally assigned to my team and as helper I took over my half of the team for caretaking; one body horse and the two wheelers. This new driver was an amiable sort who was apparently also "travelling light"; no extra clothing and attired in a blue serge suit, but wearing an O.D. army shirt. I was satisfied to resume my apprenticeship if that may be the proper term. The day the show band played their first number under the Big Top also meant the beginning of road pay for the workingmen; a few dollars more for me, plus a $10.00 holdback.

Following the D.C. date we loaded our team for the next stand; Baltimore, May 2 and 3. I had gone to bed and just before the train pulled out, Apples Welsh came bursting into our car. He was cussing as he called out, "Where is that SOB (driver's name), he is a deserter from the Army and the authorities are here to pick him up." So there went that driver, and I was once more on my own, at least for Baltimore. I was to see a frequent succession of drivers as time went on, as they were transferred, for the most part to eight-horse teams, being experienced drivers. Anyway, I knew our load assignments for the nightly tear-down. First load was #115, side-show panel wagon, so we had quite a wait till they closed down. Team stayed on the bedding until dark, then we moved outside the side show till that wagon was loaded and ready. We took it only to the street, where it was taken by the Tractors through to the train. Next load was the sideshow Light Plant #112, or #113, if I remember correctly. This entailed another wait, until the sideshow was entirely loaded. It was during this wait I had the opportunity to see the "strange people" depart for the train, being loaded into the sideshow, curtained Reo bus, driven by George Webster. Generally Eeeko and Iko managed to get seats near the door, dressed in their street attire and wearing those huge caps, covering their weird blonde curls. We took the Light Plant wagon on through to the runs, and unless ordered back to the lot for another load, we were through for the night. We rode the third (scenery) section, so-called because some of its final trip was in daylight hours, before arriving in "tomorrow's town."

In answer to your question as to which was my favorite show and since the Big One was my first, definitely Ringling-Barnum was and always will be my choice. My only other circus for comparison was Christy Bros. where I did a brief stint in the spring of 1930. I joined it in their South Houston quarters as they were preparing to load for their first opening in Galveston. Jack Morgan was Boss Hostler, and he gave me a train team to drive. That night as we prepared to leave he showed me to the car where the baggage stock men were to sleep. I had been up all the preceding night travelling to Houston so was ready to hit the hay. However, my response was short-lived. I awoke with bedbugs covering me and really getting a feast off me. I got out of there fast and headed for the flats, where I opened a bale of hay stashed there and spent the rest of the night under a wagon. I unloaded the show, made parade driving a bear cage wagon, loaded the show at night, then took off down the road. So you might say I opened and closed on the Christy Show, all in two days.

The Bosses on Ringling Circus, 1928 season: Tom Lynch, Boss Hostler, then not too active but still the boss; Henry (Apples) Welsh, First Assistant, and prince of a man; Jim Doyle, in charge of stock on the Squadron; Joe Fish (Bartholomae); Spot Griffin, Dinty Moore, Assistants; Harry Snyder, in charge of the Medicine Chest, doctoring stock; Rattlesnake Bill, in charge of the feed pile and #12 stable wagon (said to be a former Cossack Troupe member on the Bill Show); Blind Louis (Waxy) Panzer, harness maker.

I do not know the number of baggage horses on the show that year, possibly about 350 in the two large tent stables. I think the four-train sections totaled 104 cars. I came to know quite a few of the drivers and helpers; many of them dated back to the Barnum show prior to the 1919 combine and were "down-Easters," so identified by their accent.

Some old-timers I recall: Bill Fifield, Roy Ralph (he was my driver for a while until promoted to an eight); Charlie Rigsby; George O'Brien; Bill Tucker; Young Joe Williams; Mike Larkins; Red McNaul; Deafy Smith; Ted White, etc. Ted later was on the Cole Show working for Arky Scott on elephants. He was killed by the male "Joe" who crushed him to death in the bull car. I believe that was in 1943 as I was back in the Army at the time. Other six-horse drivers I knew (the foregoing were all on eights): Pete Green who generally broke a green team of colts each spring; "Two-Gun" Whitey Warner, later train master on Cole Bros.; Jack Wodehouse; "Slew-Foot" Murphy; Tom Gill; Fred Moore;

Frenchy LeBlanc; Menominee Dutch; Mishawaukee Heavy; Jimmy Colgate, etc. Jimmy was said to be a member of the Soap Colgate family. As I recall, Dave "Deacon" Blanchfield was driving a four-up stake driver team, and they called him "Blanch."

My favorite teams were the two Red Roan, eight-horse, Big Top Chain (hook rope) teams. Drivers were Denver Curly and Roy "Gunsel" Weber. There was plenty of action on their part whenever a bad lot was encountered. "The Gunsel," as he was called, was a short heavy-set man, and when his team was on a dead run after getting a mired wagon to moving, it looked like they were about to pull him over his wheeler's hames, as Gunsel pulled back on his lines.

So concluded "Spike" Hansen in his captivating and delightfully detailed firsthand account of life in the baggage stock department.

Drivers all held their lines the same way. The line from the off-leader went over the first finger and down through the driver's right hand. The line from the off six-horse body pole team went over the second finger and down through the hand. The line from the off four-horse body pole team went over the next finger, and the line from the off-wheeler went over the little finger and down. The lines from the near horses were fed through the fingers and up over the thumb of the left hand. These lines were all placed one finger lower than those held in the right hand.

The *Hagenbeck-Wallace Circus* in 1910 paid its four-horse drivers $15.00 per month and up to $50.00 per month for an eight-horse driver. They were also given their meals and a bunk for sleeping on the train.

One driver, Buffalo Gustin, reflected that a driver was paid $10.50 a week for driving a ten-horse team in the 1907 era; a six-up driver got $3.50 a week. Gustin said he only got $3.50 a week, the rest of his $10.50 pay was held back until the end of the season. This was common practice on circuses. It encouraged the men to stick it out for the full season.

Mike Tschudy, in pointing out pay schedules in the 1930s on the *Al G. Barnes Circus*, explained, "All eight-horse drivers, train team men, pull up, and pullaway drivers, feed pile men, medicine chest man, and the night watchman, all drew the pay of an eight-horse driver.

"All helpers on an eight-horse drew the same pay as a four-horse driver. Six-horse pay went to the drivers of six-up, as well as pull-over team drivers, and saddle pony boy.

"Six-horse helpers and four-horse drivers had their own rate. The pay scales were flexible so if a good man came along he could be paid a better wage."

In the period 1920 through 1925 on *Ringling Bros. and Barnum & Bailey Combined Shows* the pay scale was $14.50 a week for an eight-horse driver, his helper $9.00, $12.50 for a six-horse, and a four-horse driver $10.50. There was, in addition, a $20.00 a month hold-back paid at the end of the season.

"In the early 1930s when I was on the *Ringling Show*," said long-string driver Ed Binner, "I got $14.00 a week with a $20.00 a month hold-back. This $20.00 was collectible only if you stayed until the end of the season."

In these same years the Boss Hostler was paid $125.00 a week; his assistants $50.00 a week; blacksmiths $35.00 a week; and his helper $25.00 a week. The night watchman was paid $9.35 a week. The train team drivers were scaled $11.65 for pull-up team drivers; $9.35 pull-over team drivers. All these men had the same hold-back paid at the end of the season. In addition, everybody received three square meals a day and a place to sleep on the train.

Mike Tschudy said that on the *Al G. Barnes Circus* that each six- and eight-horse team driver had a helper. This man assisted in harnessing, care of harness, grooming, feeding, and watering. Drivers of four-ups and two-horse train teams took care of their own horses.

Route books issued by various circuses frequently carried accounts of the highlights for each day in each town. These terse statements told a great deal about the stamina of circus men, especially the long-string drivers. In the course of a season everything was not always sunny skies and grassy lots. Here are comments from a few such route books that tell much about the headaches and heartaches that occurred during the season.

1891—*Adam Forepaugh Shows.* The circus was out for 175 days and carried 173 baggage horses. Lima, Ohio—haul to the lot was two miles. Muskegon, Michigan—lot was sandy. Eau Claire, Wisconsin—lot a long way from railroad unloading. St. Paul, Minnesota—severe thunderstorm all day. Sioux City, Iowa

—lot bad. Keokuk, Iowa—lot way out. Council Bluffs, Iowa—lot bad. Colfax, Washington—lot miles away over bad roads. Dust terrible. Seattle, Washington—long haul to the lot. Tacoma, Washington—lot sandy. Olympia, Washington—a long haul to railroad cars.

1892—*Ringling Bros. Circus* had 204 baggage horses and were on the road 180 days. Monroe, Wisconsin—bottomless roads and juicy mud. The sinking fairground abandoned after pitching tents. Huron, South Dakota—5-ton bandwagon mired hub deep. Marshfield, Wisconsin—frog pond lot. Escanaba, Michigan—sandy lot, a long way out. Plattsmouth, Nebraska—lot 3 miles out in country. Dustiest and dirtiest and meanest day of the season.

1897—*Ringling Bros.*, LaSalle, Illinois—every wagon mired to the hubs, bad a lot as could be found. Freeport, Illinois—heavy thunderstorm and high winds blew down the horse tents. No damage to the horses.

1901—*Ringling Bros.*, Mansfield, Ohio—lot 2 miles from runs and one mile from town. Bethlehem, Pennsylvania—valuable horse died in the morning. Delavan looks gloomy. Two more horses died during the day. Delavan takes it much to heart as he seldom loses an animal. Boston, Massachusetts—the lot is a small ocean. Some places water is two feet deep. It has been a hard time on horses and men. Worcester, Massachusetts—the cookhouse wagon overturned and a valuable horse was killed. Ogdensburg, New York—rained all day. Parade at 10 A.M. Lot in awful condition. Tents all up then it was decided not to show as ground is so soft it was unsafe to seat immense crowd. It was late into the night when the show finally was loaded. Potsdam, New York—a heavy lot a mile out. Recent rains have made lot soft and spongy. Toronto, Ontario—good lot two miles out and a mile from runs. Parade leaves at 9:20 A.M. and returns at 11:20 A.M. Hamilton, Ontario—lot two miles from the runs and three miles from town. Cleveland, Ohio—parade at 8:30 A.M. and returns at 11:30 A.M. Ashland, Wisconsin—bad lot. Mud a foot deep. Heavy wagons sank way down. Asst. Supt. Jenkins and Boss Hostler Delavan Alexander had all kinds of trouble to get things placed. At night the lot in awful condition and it was day-

light before the last flatcar was loaded. Cookhouse wagon got ditched and there were other accidents. Perry, Oklahoma Territory—Ed "Shorty" Sharp, a four-horse driver, coming onto the lot with a heavy wagon was descending an embankment when his front wheel hit a hole, jerked wagon and threw Shorty off. He landed in front of the wagon and a wheel went over his body. *Ringling Bros.* paid for his funeral, and the people of the show raised $200.00 to pay for a tombstone.

Barnum & Bailey's 1906 route book lists these episodes that were problems to the long-string drivers. They had over 400 baggage horses: Holyoke, Massachusetts—lightning struck the pole of the horse tent during an electrical storm and injured three men. Cambridge, Ohio—pole wagon on the way to the lot broke through the planking of a bridge. Waterbury, Connecticut—the heavy stringer wagon upset enroute to the lot delaying traffic. Brakeman sustained a fractured collarbone. Ottawa, Ontario—severe storm blew down one of the horse tents. Niagara Falls, New York—a very dusty and rough lot. Ithaca, New York—lot very soft. Several wagons damaged being pulled onto the lot. McKeesport, Pennsylvania—a one-mile haul up a very steep hill to a rough and dusty lot. Owensboro, Kentucky—lot in bad condition due to heavy rains. Fulton, Kentucky—one mile haul to the lot over very muddy roads.

The speed of a walking horse is generally considered to be 3½ miles an hour. If the showgrounds were two or three miles out from town, as mentioned above, in some instances it meant the parade could take two or three hours to get to town, march around the downtown streets and return to the showgrounds.

In the course of a season, each day's chore was exactly the same for each driver, only the conditions under which he had to work surely varied. A man had to love show business to stick with it.

"One season," Jake Posey reflected, "early in my circus career I drove the big Rhino den on a little mud show. I can tell you it was no bed of roses. If it was raining I had to drive this heavy load in hub deep mud eight or ten miles. Sometimes we just did not make it. On occasion a bridge was too low and we had to take off the wheels and use rollers to get the wagon across. Other times a bridge would not hold the load and I was forced into a long detour. There were times when I was away from the show for a week. Just could not catch up with the show because of obstacles. We slept in canvas hammocks slung under the wagon—it was some protection. We fed the horses by grazing them along the road, but we had to pick grass, weeds, or branches to feed the Rhino. Sometimes we could purchase grain from farmers. As I said, a mud show was no bed of roses."

Some long-string drivers seemed to move from show to show. Perhaps they left a circus because they did not get along with their boss. Perhaps they could upgrade their job from a four-horse driver to a six-horse driver, thus up their pay. Maybe they changed to join a buddy, or it might have been to get on a show that had a better cookhouse.

"In 1913 I was on the *Ringling Show*," wrote Jack McCracken. "Charlie Rooney was boss hostler. We got into Butte, Montana, late on a Sunday from Ogden. John Winn had the old ten-horse team on pole wagon. He went through a bridge and we were delayed four hours getting it out; it was daylight before we got the show on lot so I washed harness, horses, and shined brass before breakfast. Rooney came around and complimented me on how nice the team and harness looked. That done, the helper and I went to breakfast—it was on the old red clay lot near the brickyard. When we got back from breakfast and found that five out of the eight horses had laid down and rolled in the red clay—boy was I mad. I did not stop for my pay—I just put on my coat and went to the CMSTP&P railroad yards, hopped a freight train, and never stopped till I got back to Sterling, Illinois, and caught the *Barnum & Bailey Show*. I had known and worked for Tom Lynch before and went around to see him. He was full-handed and took me over to Henry (Apples) Welsh who had the ring stock that year. He told Apples to keep me for a day or two until something opened up on baggage stock. You see them days a man could not get a team anytime he joined a show, as many drivers stayed year after year and as it happened that day, no team was open, so Apples put me on to help Pony Eddie who drove the 20-pony team in parade. Well, I helped Eddie get out in parade, but took my coat and went down to Aledo, Illinois,

where I joined the *101 Ranch*, went to work for Shorty Phillips driving the Minnie Six, it was so-called because of a blind mare named Minnie in the near lead, and I say that was the best six-horse team I ever drove as a hook rope team. They were all blacks and were a very pretty team. Minnie, the blind mare, never stumbled no matter how rough the lot."

In a letter of March 5, 1947, that Jack McCracken wrote to fellow long-string driver Spike Hansen he recalled, "You talk about walking away, I did that many times. I did put in several full seasons on the *Ringling Show* when it was wintering in Baraboo, Wisconsin, and also on *John Robinson, Hagenbeck-Wallace, 101 Ranch*, and *Buffalo Bill Shows*. I was on the *Barnum Show* at different times between 1907 and 1924. I only put in four full seasons. I liked to try others, too. One season, I think it was 1912, that Eddie Mullen and I made twelve circuses and Wild West Shows and two carnivals. We went from coast to coast three times in one season."

Henry "Apples" Welsh had a career driving horses for circuses that, while it would not be fair to say was typical, does indicate that a man with a reputation for being a good long-string driver could pretty well pick his own show. Welsh wrote a long letter to his friend Irvine Hetherington outlining his years on the shows:

I started out with the *Wallace Show* in Mitchell, South Dakota, August 26th. I stayed with the show that winter of 1892. It went under the title of *Cook & Withby* one season. Next season it went out as *Great Wallace Shows The Highest Classed Circus In The World*. I was not out in 1893. I went out with *Wallace Show* again in 1894. Stayed until 1896. In 1897 went to *Ringling Show*. In 1898 went to *Wallace Show* but closed out that fall with *Ringling Show* as driver of an eight-horse team on the Bell Wagon— next spring and from then on to spring of 1903. Charles Rooney and me were made assistants to Delavan next spring. I took charge of stock with *Floto Show*. Mike Haley was my assistant. Closed with *Barnes Show* that fall. That winter went to Sheridan, Pa., as assistant to McCoy. That spring assistant to Lynch. That was 1905. That was the last time the 40-horse team was ever hooked up. Tom Lynch and myself drove or herded them the last five times they were hooked up. I was assistant for Lynch until 1907. Went to *4-Paw-Sells*, assistant to George Stumph and closed with *Gollmar Bros.*

In 1908 went to *101 Ranch* and had charge of all the stock wild steers. We have four cattle on baggage and 120 saddle bronks, wild steers, buffalo. In 1908-09 closed East St. Louis that fall. That first year on *101* Daugherty was my assistant, then John Gering. George Ferguson was assistant for a few days in Graineys place but did not stay on. The next year Al Crisp was assistant for me. I was 1910-11 with *4-Paw-Sells Show*.

In 1912 went to *Buffalo Bill-Pawnee Bill Show* out of Trenton, N.J. John Devine was boss canvasman. He died the day we left Trenton. I closed with the *Davy Wheeler Show* that fall and went to *Sun Bros. Show*. Frank Wright alias Mustache Whitey and Clyde Smith assistant on the *Bill Show*. Whitey was assistant for me on *D-W*. I had no assistant on the *Sun Show*. I was the whole thing even the 24-hour man.

I think we made every town in Florida, little and big. We were in Key West four days. We closed down on Jan. 15th in White Springs, Florida. Then went to *Barnum Show* in 1913 to go assistant for Lynch, but McCoy put me on the ring stock. Elmer Brooks was assistant for me. Spring of 1914 went to *Wheeler Show* at Oxford, Pa. In 1915 went to *Gollmar Show*. Frank Rooney was assistant on *Wheeler Show* and him and me were assistants for old man Holland. In 1916 went to *Wheeler Bros.*, a 25-car show. Frank Rooney assistant. From there to *Cook* out of Cedar Rapids, Iowa, as 24-hour man. From there to *Barnum Show* to close season. Went to *Patterson-Gollmar Show* same fall at Paola, Kansas, took care of stock. Elmer Brooks was assistant for me for second time on *Barnum Shows*. Jim Babcock started out with me in 1917 but did not last long. Next winter went to Peru, Indiana, and took Robinson stock but did not go on the road. Went to West Baden, Indiana, took ring stock with *H-W Show*. Quit that show in Cincinnati and went to Chicago. I received a wire from Fred Buchanan up in Iowa to come on and buy some horses and trade some old ones that he had. After I was there a couple of months he wished the stock on me at Rapid City, South Dakota, that was in 1918. I had his stock again in 1919-20 and '21. I was at the *Sparks Show* at Macon, Georgia. 1922 to Paola, Kansas, Bert with Germain, Blackie Williamson.

Johnny was with me on the *Robinson Show*. Hughie Corrigan, Geo. Kerns, and Blackie Diller were my assistants. The *Sparks Show* was the only show I ever saw and was with it that had new stock- and flatcars in two seasons; in 1920 wooden; and in 1921 all steel. He sold his stocks and flats and all his harness to Downie. I never seen or heard of anything like it before. I was the one to spring the electric lights there on the stocks and flats. In 1922 I went from the *Patterson Buchanan Show* to the *Barnes Show* and

took the ring stock job. I joined them in Oregon and left them in Denver, Colorado. I got a wire from Mr. Mugivan to come on and take the stock on the *Robinson Show*. That fall I went to Des Moines and saw Fred Buchanan and he was trying to buy the show at Ft. Dodge, Iowa. "I will tell Mike Golden and you look out for that stock, and if I buy it I want you to look out for all the stuff until spring, then we will move it to Granger." He did not get it as Mike went to California and got money to take it out, but I did not go with it. Did not look safe to me, so I went out on a 10,000 acre ranch in northwestern Iowa. The Adams Ranch, the founder of the Adams Express Co. I left there that fall and went to California and went to work in an oil field. I had a good job, but I heard from Chas. Ringling and went to Bridgeport that spring as assistant to Lynch. I was there for six years, and if Chas. had been living I don't think I would have left them. We lost a friend when we lost him. The next spring I went to Peru, Indiana, as assistant for Chas. Rooney. Then I went to the *101 Ranch* and stayed there until 1931. Joined the *Barnes Show* and was there with them on the Medicine Box four seasons. I got sick and had a little money and the doctors got it; then I went over to go with Brown on the *Hagenbeck-Wallace Show* but got sick again, and when I got out Watts told me he wanted me to stay there as watchman in the quarters. So one day before they went out of here I got a wire forwarded from Wyoming by my brother. It was from Pat Valdo *Ringling Show* wanting to know if I would take the ring stock in the Garden, so Watts gets the wire first and brings it out to me and says, "I don't want you to go out there. I will wire them you can't come." That was a bad move I made. I could have held that job down just as well as the winter Garden job. Not as much work, but let him talk me out of it. I lost a $40.00 per week job to stay on at $10.00 per. George Smith has me in line if the job is open again. They are rather good friends of mine.

Your friend,
Henry Welsh

Ed Binner commented on switching shows: "I don't think anyone switched shows to get more money. As you know, some shows were rag bag outfits and some were real nice. As a general rule, they all fed real good. I have always said that the *Sells-Floto* fed the best of any show. At least we had steak more often.

"As far as getting a team is concerned, if you stayed on a show long enough there would be an opening. This did not hold true in the early '30s, as I recall only two drivers quitting the show in

1932, that was *Ringlings*. I do not know how many left in 1933, as I was the first to leave that year."

Will Brock had been driving long-string teams for thirty-five years. After he retired he got the itch to go back on the road "for just one season," he told his wife. She retorted, "It is alright with me, but you can make up your mind to stay with the red wagons for you will find another mule in your stall when you return." Brock wrote this to a long-time friend, Fay Reed, but he added, "Of course, my wife never said that but that was the way she felt."

Jim Traver commented, "It was an insult to a good driver to split his team. One year on the *Ringling Show* assistant Boss Hostler Rooney ordered me to split my eight into two fours, so we could take two cages to the lot. I quit in disgust and told Rooney to take his damn team and split it into eight one-horse hitches, as that was the only way he could get them to the lot was by leading them one at a time. Well, when I cooled off the boss, Old Del, talked me into staying, but he let me keep my eight."

Over the years circuses varied in size. An overland show using horse power might move from hamlet to hamlet on two or three wagons. The larger the show, of course, the more wagons and more draft horses. Likewise, shows that moved by railroad varied in size from two-car shows to 15, 30, 60, and 90 cars. The more cars the bigger the show; therefore, the need for more baggage stock. A good idea of the size and scope of a circus can be determined by the number of men in the draft horse department. In 1863 on the *Gardner & Hemming's Great American Circus*, Henry Baldwin was Boss Hostler. Under him he had a ten-horse driver and eight other men. This was a wagon show that moved overland.

The *John B. Doris Circus* of 1886 was a 35-car railroad show. Bob Abrams was Superintendent of Horses. He had one assistant, three six-horse drivers, five four-horse drivers, and twelve cage drivers that probably drove two horses on a cage.

The *Barnum & Bailey* railroad circus of 1888 listed the show as having 210 horses. There were 40 baggage wagons, 47 parade wagons and cages, and a few other assorted vehicles like ticket wagons.

In 1891 the *Adam Forepaugh Circus* moved on 48 railroad cars. This show had 173 baggage horses, 36 baggage wagons, 22 parade wagons, and one ticket wagon. Wm. J. Connor was the Boss Hostler and he had two assistants, one veterinarian, two twelve-horse drivers, five eight-horse drivers, nine six-horse drivers, twenty four-horse drivers, and four two-horse drivers on the train teams.

Another overland show was *W.B. Reynolds* in 1892. The Boss Hostler was Dick Hosler. He had one assistant and thirty-one drivers, each handling a different wagon, but each driving the same wagon every night. Scott Wickett drove the pole wagon, probably using eight or ten horses; while Pete Burns drove a four-horse, for example.

Eighteen hundred ninety-two was the ninth season the *Ringling Bros.* were in business. Their first year out, 1884, they rented horses from farmers. By 1892 they were a fine 31-railroad car show. Spencer "Delavan" Alexander was the Boss Hostler. He had two assistants, a blacksmith, harness maker, wagon repairer, wagon greaser, master of trappings and assistant, forage master, superintendent of stock loading, six stable men, four eight-horse drivers, five six-horse drivers, twenty-one four-horse drivers, and three two-horse train team drivers.

In 1901 Spencer Alexander was still the Boss Hostler for *Ringling Bros.* He had two assistants. The crew was made up of nine eight-horse drivers, ten six-horse drivers, and thirty-nine four-horse drivers and helpers. Alexander also had George Hahn as superintendent of lead bars.

Nineteen hundred five was the first year the *Carl Hagenbeck Trained Wild Animal Show* was on the road. The Boss Hostler was W.W. Scott and his assistant was John Horgan. To move the show they had two eight-horse teams, seven six-horse teams, and sixteen four-horse teams; also some train teams and probably 130 head of baggage stock.

When the *John Robinson Show* played Wheeling, West Virginia, on May 9, 1923, over one inch of snow fell. Nevertheless, Charley Rooney, Boss Hostler, got the show on the lot in time for the matinee. He had three eight-ups, five six-ups, six four-ups, and four train teams that season.

Jim Irvin, Boss Hostler, and his assistants Steve Finn and Jim

Howard, moved the *101 Ranch Real Wild West Show* during the 1925 season with one ten-horse team, two eight-horse teams, three six-horse teams, four four-horse teams, four train teams, and one extra team for hook roping wagons.

The baggage stock department, like others on the circus, seemed to enjoy the use of nicknames. These endearing monikers came about in varied and ordinary ways. Will Brock explains his:

> When *Ringling Bros.* was playing my hometown, Cedar Rapids, Iowa, I went out to the lot and talked to the Boss Hostler, Spencer Alexander. He said if I showed up the next spring in Baraboo, Wisconsin, winter quarters, he would give me a tryout. So the next spring when I got to Baraboo, I was put on grooming draft horses. I was working on a young horse with winter hair as long as your fingers and matted with manure dried in like cement. I was hard at work cuffing this shaggy horse when someone called, "Hey you." There were many men in the barn grooming these horses, so I paid no attention. "Hey you, new man," but I kept digging at the matted hair as there were other new men around. Then I heard, "Hey, Cedar Rapids, go out in the yard and help with that eight." Well then I knew it was me being yelled at, and from that moment my name was Cedar Rapids—no more Will around that show.

It was easy to guess how some names were acquired such as Broken Jaw Smitty, Roman Nose Dutch, Carrot Red, Irish Martin, or Nosey Monroe, but there were others whose origins went to the graves with their owners—Magazine Red, Cow O'Connell, Six-fingers Scotty, FewClothes Wolverton, Pile-em-up King, White Line Johnson, Feed Pete Dutch, Grandma Gardner, Gummie Smith, or Tar Heel.

The first year the five Ringling Bros. had a circus was 1884. They used horses and wagons they rented from farmers and livery stables to haul their tiny show to the next town. At the end of the season they hit the road for the winter with their *Classic &*
Comic Opera Company, playing in halls in small towns through Illinois, Iowa, Nebraska, and Wisconsin. While in Iowa in December they found a team of horses they could buy for $50.00 from a farmer. They were congratulating themselves on their bargain as they took the horses into the town's livery stable. The hostler looked the team over and advised the Ringlings that the team was spavined, had ringbone, stringhalt heaves, and, in addition, were as old as Methuselah. The Ringlings boarded the team there saying they would pick them up in the spring. Alf T. Ringling drew the honor of getting their first baggage horses. In April he took the train to Iowa, got the team, and started for Baraboo, Wisconsin. It was a dismal, miserable trip. The horses were so stove up he could not ride them. It was a slow walk to central Wisconsin. This, no doubt, was Alf T. Ringling's only experience with circus baggage stock. If he had an interest in horses it was squelched on this trip. Alf T. ended up handling advertising and publicity for the circus, as it grew into a formidable show.

In retirement in 1947, long-string driver Jack McCracken summed up his feelings to fellow driver Spike Hansen: "Yes, the old circus days as we trouped them are over and are just history, but if I had my life to live over I would do the same over again, providing there was baggage stock. There never was anything to beat a nice bunch of horses pulling the big red, iron-tired wagons. This motorized age has ended that, but as it is now, it is far from the old thrill and glamor that used to be with the horses."

In the 1920s and 1930s it became more and more difficult to find drivers who could handle long-string circus teams. Driving horses on a farm or commercial drayage work in a city did not train a man for circus work except as to the care of and the handling of horses. The shortage of long-string drivers went hand in hand with the shortage of good drafters and no doubt had much to do with the decision to switch from Percherons to "*Cats* and *Macks.*"

Jake Posey, Boss Hostler, on the black horse, and Waxey Olson, the harness maker, of the 1915 Hagenbeck-Wallace Circus. *Author's Collection.*

Photo taken July 5, 1929 on the Ringling lot in Hartford, Connecticut, shows three veterans—Lewis Marshall, Tom Lynch, Boss Hostler in center, and Red Finn. *Circus World Museum, Baraboo, Wisconsin.*

Jake Posey drove the 40-horse hitch for Barnum & Bailey in Europe at the turn of the century. Later he was Boss Hostler for Buffalo Bill's Wild West Show, Sparks Circus in the 1920s, and Al G. Barnes Circus in the early 1930s. *Circus World Museum, Baraboo, Wisconsin.*

Tom Lynch was Boss Hostler for Barnum & Bailey, then later for the Combined Shows of Ringling Bros. and Barnum & Bailey until he retired in 1934. This photo of Lynch was taken on the lot at Erie, Pennsylvania, June 21, 1924. Lynch knew his stock well and is credited with knowing the names of all of his horses and where they fit in a team. *Frank Updegrove Photo.*

Red Finn was the last Boss Hostler on Ringling Bros. and Barnum & Bailey Circus. When the show went back to winter quarters in 1938, the drafters were sold and Finn's job no longer existed. *John Zweifel Collection.*

Boss Hostler for Cole Bros. Circus in 1940 was Joe Wallace. Seen here on his pinto Joe was the last Boss for this show, because at the end of the season they sold their baggage stock. *Harold Gorsuch Photo.*

Blackie Dill was an assistant Boss Hostler on the Ringling Circus in 1925 when this photo was taken in Greenwood, Mississippi. *Frank Updegrove Photo.*

Left: Spencer Alexander was Boss Hostler for Ringling Bros. in 1893. He was nicknamed "Delavan" because he came from that town in southern Wisconsin. Right: Bob Meek was assistant Boss Hostler for Ringling Bros. in 1893. *Both photos from Author's Collection.*

On the Sells-Floto Circus, 1926. In the group from left to right are Jake; Ed Binner; Pony Cleland; Charlie Gott, blacksmith; Harry Lott, assistant Boss Hostler; Jerry Wade, horseshoer; Heavy Higgins, third assistant Boss Hostler; and George, blacksmith's helper. *Ed Binner Collection.*

A group of drivers and helpers on the 1926 Sells-Floto Circus. Ed Binner is on the right in the back row. *Ed Binner Collection.*

Two eight-horse drivers still with The Greatest Show On Earth in 1953, fifteen years after the draft stock were sold. Now bosses in the ring stock department, Frank Warner and Harold Miller in rig, discuss a problem on the Dayton, Ohio, lot. *Harold Gorsuch Photo.*

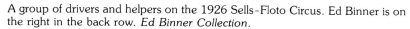

Harry Baker started his circus career driving a team for Sun Bros. in 1893. Later he was with John Robinson, and in 1903 he went with Ringling Bros. as a long-string driver. He stayed with the big show through 1938, when they sold all their draft stock to drive teams in the performance spec. *Author's Photo.*

The 1895 drivers for Ringling Bros. Circus. They answer to names like Tollworth, Meek, McCall, Moran, Lynch, Walters, Lewis, McCafferty, Clark, or Hall. On the circus lot they are more apt to answer to Slim, Red, Dago, Omaha, 101, Shorty, Frenchy, or Blackie. *Author's Collection.*

The little sign on the wall says, "Men who know it all are not invited." Henry Moeller on the left put up the sign in his tiny office, where old-timers around Baraboo, Wisconsin, would stop in to talk politics or circus. Henry, his brother Corwin, and his father, Henry, Sr., ran a wagon shop. Here they produced vehicles of all types and styles for their cousins the Ringlings and Gollmars, and many other circuses. On this February day in 1953, Henry's argument was with Jim "Mushmouth" Traver, old-time Ringling eight-horse driver. They were trying to pin the blame on each other for knocking the busts off the wood-carved figures on the side of the Germany wagon. Moeller said Traver couldn't drive the team in a tight place, meaning the door into the shop. Traver insisted that Moeller, who was directing the operation, got him too close to the door frame. *Author's Photo.*

Dick Sells making a right turn onto the lot at Minneapolis, August 2, 1925. The Percherons nimbly swing wide around the corner, never getting fouled up in trace chains, dragging body poles, or lead bars. Fellow driver Ed Binner said of Dick Sells, "He was an excellent linesman. He made the team what it was. In other words, he could improve even a poor team."

Dick Sells was one of Ringling's better drivers. Here he swings his eight Percherons onto the Memphis lot, October, 28, 1924. #43 Wagon carries the 62-foot-long center poles. *Frank Updegrove Photo.*

From the drivers seat, a 6-up looks like this. A good straight line, all horses are pulling evenly on this slight upgrade on the way to the Ardmore, Oklahoma, lot in 1924. Ringling Bros. and Barnum & Bailey Circus. *Frank Updegrove Photo.*

An excellent view of an 8-up driver, Ringling Bros. and Barnum & Bailey, 1936. *Circus World Museum, Baraboo, Wisconsin.*

The camera caught this scene at the instant the driver was signaling the team to swing right and go into the lot. The brakeman has his stick in the brake wheel, giving him extra leverage to control the forward movement of #82 Wagon. One of the Boss Hostlers is just crossing the sidewalk and directing the driver where to go. The little boy in the street in the lower left corner is in a precarious spot, not realizing that the leaders will be swinging right around where he is standing. Sells-Floto, 1925. *Author's Collection.*

Eight dapple grey Percherons move a heavy wagon up a slight grade. The wheelers are a bit slow in getting into action. Ringling Show, 1938, at Dayton, Ohio. *Harold Gorsuch Photo.*

Swinging an eight-horse team around a corner requires great skill. Here the heavily loaded Commissary Department wagon makes it with ease. Newark, New Jersey, 1936. As usual, the hame is used as a coatrack. This is a fine team of grade Belgians. *Circus World Museum, Baraboo, Wisconsin.*

A first-rate eight-horse team of roan Belgian horses taking a cookhouse wagon to the runs in the late afternoon. The leaders, out of the photo, are not doing any pulling, as the body pole can be seen dragging. *Circus World Museum, Baraboo, Wisconsin.*

A hard pull with a heavy load. This driver has his team well strung out and pulling evenly. Note the coat hanging on the hame of the near horse in the four-horse body pole team. Hames were about the only place where a driver could keep his rain gear or coat. On a circus, an eight like this was made up of the wheelers, four-horse body pole team, six-horse body pole team, and the leaders. The 6-up on the hillside is standing by to act as a chain team to move a particularly heavy wagon up the incline. RBB&B, Paterson, New Jersey, 1936. *Circus World Museum, Baraboo, Wisconsin.*

A 4-up moves a light cage toward the menagerie tent on the Al G. Barnes-Sells Floto Circus in 1938. *Joe Fleming Collection.*

Stock Department

Jake Posey	Boss Hostler
Steve Brown	Asst. Boss Hostler
Blackie Johnson	Feed Pile
Bert Warner	Stock Watchman
Lou Martin	No. 1 Band Team
Blackie Norris	No. 2 Band Team
Johnnie Wright	Eight Horse Driver
Tommie Sawyer	No. 1 Hook Rope Team
Curly Schultz	No. 2 Hook Rope Team

6 Horse Drivers

Whitie Peterson	E. C. Kurkwood
Claude Davis	Dutch Feusic

Dutch Feusic, Traffic Officer and Lead Bar Supt.

Frank Gar	Four Horse Team
Eddie Anderson	Four Horse Team
J. W. Murray	Pullover Team
Martin Beamish	Pullover Team
John J. Welsh	Pullup Team

Eight Horse Helpers

Robert Duke	Bob McBride

Six Horse Helpers

Richard Samler	Bill Hoffman
Roy Bryn	Jim Steward
	Ralph Rothrock

The Sparks Circus listed these men in their 1927 Route Book as the "Stock Department." *Author's Collection.*

Baggage Stock Department.

THOMAS LYNCH,	. . . . Superintendent
JOHN KUHLMANN,	. . . . First Assistant
GEORGE FERGUSON,	. . . . Second Assistant
HENRY WELSH,	. . . . Third Assistant
HENRY SWIFT,	. . . . in charge of Feed
RUDOLF MERTZ,	. . . . Veterinary
FRANK WOARD,	. . . . Hospital Stock
GEORGE HAHN,	. . . . Lead Bars
WILLIAM STILLMAN,	. . . Night Watchman
ARTHUR CLARK,	. . . . Night Watchman

DRIVERS.

EIGHT-HORSE DRIVERS AND HELPERS.

Frank Aults,	John Duff,
William Fifield,	Thomas McCarthy,
James McGuffin,	Edward Halfaker,
Myron Bullard,	Joseph Wagner,
Joseph Williams,	Walter Hower,
John Granz,	Charles Haley,
David Denio,	Samuel Pike,
Harry Whitney,	William McCoy,
James Johnson,	William Tooley,
James McPherson,	Henry Neall,
John Winn,	Frank Layfield,
Burton Warner,	Richard Method
John Buttermore,	John Kelker.

SIX-HORSE.

John Lewis,	John Martin,
William Golse,	Joseph Kerper,
Eugene Knowlton,	Clark Smith,
William Lunger,	John Pinion,
Walter Manning,	Charles Barnard,
Charles Haley,	John Meade,
Samuel Walker,	Frank Speidell,
Eli Fournier,	Charles Corder.
William Larin,	

The baggage stock department for Barnum & Bailey in 1906. *Author's Collection.*

FOUR-HORSE.

John Wilcox,	George Fought,
John Minick,	George Curran,
James Shehan,	Patrick Briggs,
James McDonnell,	Martin Haley,
James McDermott,	Charles Grant,
John Partridge,	Albert Myers,
Frank Neuman,	James Budrose,
Charles Baultz,	Frederick Wellington,
Harold Bailey,	Alfred Cyr,
John Woods,	Edward Shaw,
Henry Jooris,	Herbert Wimer.

PULL-OVER DRIVERS.	PULL-UP DRIVERS.
Charles Cook,	Charles Norn,
Grant Nolvey,	George Minan.
William Staats,	WATER-CART DRIVER.
Charles Churn.	Julius Porter.

Blacksmith Shop.

DANIEL TAYLOR, ... Superintendent

HEAD HORSESHOER.	HORSESHOER.
J. B. Spears.	Henry McQuillian.
FLOORMEN.	REPAIR BLACKSMITHS.
Pat. O'Hara,	Alexander Young,
Charles F. Turnley,	Joseph Doyle.
Joseph S. Henderson.	

CARPENTER, Otto Eiermann.

Oilers.

James Ferraro,	Con. Shay.

Harnessmakers.

Charles Olson,	J. Ernst Simpson.

Two circuses needed long-string drivers early in the season, resulting in these ads in *Billboard*, May 15, 1926. *Author's Collection.*

BAGGAGE STOCK.

S. ALEXANDER........ ......Superintendent.
ROBERT MEEK................. ..Assistant.
Fred Turner.......... ....Blacksmith
George Hall........ ....Blacksmith
Harry Scott... ....Blacksmith
Edward Ihler..................... ....Wagon Repairer
Dave Miller..........................Harness Maker
Frank Eddle...... ....Greaser
Ed. Farley...... ....Watchman
John Richards... ....Watchman

EIGHT-HORSE DRIVERS.

| Robert Meek. | Byron Wilson. | Dave Shane. |
| Harry Moran. | Joe Hanna. | James Clary. |

SIX-HORSE DRIVERS.

Roy Dunbar.	John Peterson.	Wm. Allen.
Peter Simmons.	Sam Woodman.	Nick Stevens.
Wm. Hill.	Robt. Milford.	Leonard Barnes.
Chas. Baldwin.	Pony Wilson.	

FOUR-HORSE DRIVERS.

Chas. Lindsay.	Ed. Louis.	Carl Cushing.
Edward Pope.	Mike Kelly.	Frank Gross.
Tom Dorsey.	Cal. Nordyar.	Ed. Feldon.
John Born.	George Robinson.	John Roney.
Wm. Hanlon.	John Carlson.	Frank Evans.
Otto Ziegler.	Geo. Smith.	Doc Conners.
Joe Blaze.	Frank Burst.	Milton Gilpatrick.
Ed. Lawrence.		

HELPERS.

J. Anderson.	John Shuler.	John Sanders.
Omer Crontz.	Tom Pope.	Joe Luth.
John Davis.	Henry Lee.	Henry Larkins.
Victor Tuttle.	Geo. Wright.	Geo. Ryan.

PULL-UP TEAM MEN.

| George Williams. | Ed. Laysey. | Archie Phillips. |
| Albert Crandell. | L. Purves. | |

STABLE MEN.

Wm. Crosby.	Sam Smith.	Harry Clapper.
Hamilton Brown.	Isaac Duell.	Wm. Vangarder.
John Bishop.	Ed. Jones.	Geo. Ryland.
Sherman Pennington.		

The 1895 baggage stock department for Ringling Bros., World's Greatest Shows. *Author's Collection.*

In September 1906, the Barnum & Bailey Show seemed to be shorthanded enough to place this ad in *Billboard* magazine. Tom Lynch was explicit in his wants. *Author's Collection.*

WANTED, FOR THE
BARNUM & BAILEY
GREATEST SHOW ON EARTH

For the next Spring season in Madison Square Garden, New York City, and for the Second Summer Tour of the country (during 1904) since its return from five years' absence in Europe,

THE SOLID CREAM OF THE WHOLE WORLD'S ATTRACTIONS.

Nothing can possibly be either too grand or too costly, so that they are absolutely the best, they will do; and this means everything that can be used for exhibition under canvas, whether

PERFORMERS, SPECIALTIES, ANIMALS, PRODIGIES OR OTHER FEATURES.

The exalted character, fine unrivalled reputation, vast financial resources, massive, grand and expensive outfit of this now WORLD FAMOUS SHOW,

IMPERATIVELY DEMANDS THE HIGHEST GRADE ACTS AND ARTISTS.

And these are what are now sought, and for which the highest salaries commensurate with the merit of the attraction and skill and standing of the artists will be cheerfully paid, if found suitable.

THEREFORE, THERE ARE WANTED

Educational Objects, Instructive Exhibits, Meritorious Novelties, Children's Attractions, Sensational Acts, Starling Features, High Class Specialties and the Choicest Kinds of Skilled and Expert Performances.

THE FINEST MALE AND FEMALE PERFORMERS IN ALL LINES.

Single, Double, Triple, in Troupes, Groups or Whole Companies: Acrobats, Gymnasts, Tumblers, Leapers, Vaulters, Somersaulters and Originators; Clowns, Comic Sketches, Grotesque Acts, High Kickers, Fantastiques, Singers, Dancers, Musicians and Inventors; Jockeys, Trainers, Teachers, Experts, Menage Artists, Horsemen of all degrees, Arenic Actors and Exploiters; Freaks, Prodigies, Curiosities, Sports, Oddities, Animal Wonders and Animate and Inanimate Marvels.

THE HIGHER CLASS THE FEATURE THE MORE IT IS SUITABLE.

As the avowed aim and settled determination are to increase the Largest and Greatest Show on Earth and place it upon an elevated plane of stupendous grandeur hitherto deemed impossible, by immensely augmenting each and every department to enormous proportions with

ALL THE BEST PERFORMERS AND HIGH CLASS ATTRACTIONS OBTAINABLE.

For nothing less can possibly satisfy the exacting and critical communities of New York City, and other Great Capitals, before whom this Show, and this Show only, gives exclusive exhibitions.

To economize time and save duplicate correspondence, Artists are requested to furnish, in first letter, a full and complete description of their act or acts, number of persons in troupe, what apparatus or properties (if any) they have, lowest salary, and forward photographs in costume. Equestrians owning their stock given a preference.

ALSO WANTED, BANDSMEN AND MUSICIANS.

50 Skilled Musicians to augment the several Military Bands.

ALSO WANTED, FOR THE ADVANCE,

Car Managers, Agents, Boss Bill Posters, Contracting Agents in all lines, Bill Posters, Lithographers, Checker Up, Route Riders, Car Cooks and Porters, and these must be of good character, trustworthy and reliable. To all these the best wages will be paid, and if found competent a season's engagement will be offered.

ALSO WANTED,

Assistant Foremen and Workingmen of all grades, Canvas Men, Seat Men, Railroad Men, Property and Wardrobe Men, Chandelier Men, Stable Men, Grooms, Animal and Elephant Keepers, Wheelwrights, Blacksmiths, Horseshoers, and 4, 6, 8 and 10 Horse Drivers. Careful and painstaking men in these several positions will be appreciated, well recompensed and well provided for in every way, and when found capable and efficient promoted as occasion justifies.

All business communications and applications from Artists should be addressed to

JAMES A. BAILEY, General Manager.

James A. Bailey wanted for his Greatest Show on Earth, season of 1904, stablemen, wheelwrights, blacksmiths, horseshoers, and 4, 6, 8, and 10-horse drivers. From the *New York Clipper*, October 31, 1903. *Author's Collection.*

In this 1937 photo, many special circus features can be seen. Note the corner bull ring and side bull ring for hook roping on a soft lot. The big gooseneck on the end of the wagon pole is clearly seen. Note the ladder rungs on the side of the wagon and the side racks for carrying equipment. A body pole rests on hooks. *Circus World Museum, Baraboo, Wisconsin.*

CHAPTER 3

The Wagons

On any circus there were two classifications of wagons, parade and baggage. Parade wagons frequently carried baggage, but baggage wagons were rarely paraded. The parade wagons will be discussed and illustrated in a later chapter. Here we will cover, mainly, the baggage wagons that the circus draft horses had to pull from the railroad unloading area (the "runs" as this area was called) to the showgrounds over city streets and onto the lot, regardless of ground conditions, where the horses spotted the wagons in their proper locations.

One could almost say all circus wagons were unique. They differed in dimensions of length, width, height, open or closed top, racks, and hooks on the sides, diameter and width of wheels, and the heft built into the undercarriage. Some had possum bellies of varying sizes, and some carried spare wheels. Rarely were any two wagons identical. Each was designed and built for the particular load it was to carry.

In the commercial field during the horse-drawn era, companies that manufactured, for example, express or beer wagons, offered in their catalogs vehicles that could haul loads of various sizes. Such vehicles spent 100 percent of their working life on the paved streets of the cities. When it came to a circus baggage wagon, the problem was different. The circus always had to build a vehicle to withstand the worst possible conditions.

From the runs to the lot going over paved streets no problem existed. Two, or perhaps four, draft horses could move any wagon. But when the wagon moved off the street onto the lot which, perhaps, was loose sand, then the wagons and the horses met the acid test.

If the six- or eight-horse team could not keep the vehicle moving, other long-string teams were hooked on the wagon and it was spotted. The wagon had to hold together. It was overengineered for this reason. These vehicles were a remarkable memorial to ingenuity and craftsmanship of the circus wagon builders.

For years before and after the turn of the century there were commercial wagon makers that contracted for building circus vehicles. Generally, after 1920, when the horse-drawn era was close to the end, these wagon works disappeared. The circuses then took on the job of building specialized wagons in their own winter quarters' shops.

Charley Lucky was in charge for the American Circus Corporation Shows, including *John Robinson Circus* and *Hagenbeck-Wallace Circus*. Bill Yeske did the job for *Ringling Bros.* and *Barnum & Bailey*. Cap Curtis handled it for *Sells-Floto Circus*.

Each winter *Billboard Magazine* would report activity at the various circus quarters. Frequently mention would be made of what was going on in the wagon shops—Granger, Iowa, *Robbins Bros. Circus*, January 1925: "Earl Sinnott, Superintendent, has extra wagons under construction, including a new Calliope and

Bandwagon." Peru, Indiana, *Hagenbeck-Wallace Circus*, February 1923: "Charley Brady, in charge of the Wagon Shop at the circus farm and his crew are getting the cages and baggage wagons ready."

Macon, Georgia, *Sparks Circus*, January 1925: "The blacksmith and woodworking departments are under the direction of Sailor Holcomb with those two old-timers, Pop Coy and Gary Vanderbilt as assistants." Beaumont, Texas, *Christy Bros. Circus*, January 1925: "Remarkable progress has been made in the construction of the new dens and baggage wagons, and Ike Ellis who is in charge of this department has 12 worthy woodworkers and painters busy with four blacksmiths making music at the forges."

Camp Knox, Kentucky, *Walter L. Main Circus*, February 1928: "In the last 60 days four new baggage wagons have been built." Sarasota, Florida, *Ringling Bros. and Barnum & Bailey Circus*, December 1928: "The first 32 wagons have been turned forth from the wagon shop where William Yeske superintends. The work and the blueprints for the new giraffe wagons and other new cages and wagons to be turned out are now in the hands of the Wagon Shop. Work is at least 50% further ahead in this Department than at this time last season. Several new cages are to be built to care for the additions to the menagerie next season. Yeske has a full crew of men working under his direction."

Granger, Iowa, *Robbins Bros. Circus*, January 1926: "Joe Bullington, Master Mechanic, is supervising building of the new wagons. A new seal den, stake driver, canvas wagon, property wagon, as well as overhauling a dozen or more other large wagons. Blackie Jack Kane, Boss Hostler, is keeping the drafters in good shape."

Louisville, Kentucky, *Walter L. Main*, March 1926: "M.G. Smith, Superintendent of the Wagon Shop, is equipping all the baggage wagons with a new brake. The heavier wagons have a double set of brakes on the rear wheels."

The wagons were not cumbersome and unwieldy. They could be loaded onto the circus train of flatcars quickly and easily, unloaded with the same dispatch. They could almost turn on a dime because the front wheels could always cut under the body of the wagon.

On the largest wagons, the fifth wheel was made of 5/8-inch thick by 2-inch wide flat stock, with a diameter of 55 or 57 or even 59 inches.

All were equipped with heavy bull rings of steel on each corner. Some wagons that carried exceptionally heavy loads, or were extra long, had bull rings located on each side. These rings had a threefold use. They were used for loading the wagon on the flatcar; that is, pulling it up the runs and across the string of flats. They were also used to unload the wagons. Thirdly, they were used on soft lots. Extra chain teams or hook rope teams used the bull rings to assist in moving the wagons.

Every wagon was equipped with a brake system, either hand operated or foot operated, that applied pressure of brake shoes to the rear wheels.

When the wagons were moving over city streets to and from the showgrounds, hills were encountered. Generally speaking, lightweight wagons, such as cages, had foot-operated brakes, while the big vehicles were equipped with hand-operated brakes —the kind used on a boxcar—that gave the brakeman more leverage. In some towns the show had to navigate steep hills that put the brakes to maximum use. Some of the more massive wagons had double brakes; that is, shoes that clamped both front and back surfaces of the rear wheels.

The show could not function on the pleasant thought of "wait until the sun shines, then we will move the circus off the muddy lot." No matter how hard it rained, nor how muddy the lot was in Milwaukee, the circus had to tear down, load the wagons, load the train, and move ninety miles north to Green Bay because the show was advertised to play there the next day. This type of discipline required the circuses to be self-sufficient. To achieve this goal, first and foremost the wagons had to hold together under adverse conditions. There was plenty of Percheron power to move the wagons, so they were always built to take a beating. One example of the massiveness built into these vehicles is the construction of the pole (the tongue, as it is known to noncircus people).

These 11½-foot long poles gave a tremendous leverage. If the front wheels were sunk in sand or mud, these poles would be easy to snap off when turning. To eliminate that potential problem, the poles were always big and heavy. Many were 12¼ inches wide and 3 to 4 inches thick and reinforced with strap iron. Another example was the axle. These were steel forgings anywhere from 2½ inches square up to 4 inches square and 8 feet long.

Probably the wheels were the most beautifully engineered part of a circus baggage wagon. One of the foremost sources of these enormous wheels was St. Marys, Ohio, where the St. Marys Wheel & Spoke Company was located. Mr. J.C. White was Superintendent and his father, Thomas A. White, was President and General Manager from about 1890 to 1936. St. Marys had the reputation of manufacturing the finest, sturdiest, and most reliable wheels of any size a circus required. Mr. White explained how these massive circus wheels were made:

> The hubs were always made of elm because of its toughness. After they were turned and mortised to fit the flanges, the spokes were driven into the hub blocks, then the Sarven flanges were pressed on hydraulically. The spokes were white oak and were turned to desired diameter and mortised to fit right in the hub. The other end of the spoke was tenoned to fit the felloe. Before assembling, the spokes were sanded and finished. They were also grooved for the 5/16-inch panels that were inserted between the spokes. The spokes were then driven into the hub, filed, sanded, and finished in the center of the wheel. The panels were then glued in place before the felloes were applied. The felloes were white oak. (The panels mentioned were for sunburst wheels used on parade wagons.)
>
> All wood used was air-dried in open sheds for about two years before using. After this the billets were dried to about 4 percent moisture content in the dry kilns. The dish was built into the wheels by the angle we put on the tennon that was driven into the hub.
>
> The steel tire was shrunk on the wheel as a last step. When finished, the wheels were dipped in linseed oil.

Mr. White concluded by saying that they discovered that after the wheels were in service, the moisture content in the wood rose to 14 to 16 percent, which would cause the wood to swell. This, in turn, tightened the entire assembly held within the heavy steel tire, making it tour-worthy for many years.

In mid-season in 1938 the labor unions tied up the *Ringling Bros. and Barnum & Bailey Circus* with strikes, sending the great show back to winter quarters. This was the end of the draft horses for this circus. The following year elephants, *Mack* trucks, and *Caterpillar* tractors moved the show on and off the lot.

To illustrate the great variety of wagons and their loads used by the *Ringling Circus* during 1937, its last full year with Percheron power, the major vehicles are listed herewith:

Wagon Number	Length (ft./in.)	Load
1	16	Cookhouse Tables
2	16	Boiler Wagon
3	16	Refrigerator Wagon
4	18	Nonperishable Food
5	17	Dining Dept. Tables
6	18	Oven Wagon
7	18	Oven Wagon
8	20	Dining Dept. Tent
9	18	Blacksmith Shop
10	20	Canvas for 2 Baggage Stock Tents
11	20	Stakes & Poles for Baggage Stock Tents
12	18	Horse Trappings
13	16	Menagerie Stake & Chain
14	20	Commissary
15	30	Menagerie Poles & Stakes
16	13/6	Seat Planks
17	13/6	Seat Planks
18,19,20	19	Chairs
21-27	18	Bible Backs-Seats
28,29	20	Jacks for Seats
30	15	Ring Curbs & Carpenter Shop
31	32/6	Grandstand Stringers
32,33	30	Stringers
34	32/6	Grandstand Stringers

Wagon Number	Length (ft./in.)	Load
35	15	Extra Seats
36	15	Performers Rigging
38	16	Big Top Stake & Chain
39	18	Big Top Stake & Chain
40	18/6	Rigging & Side Poles
41	18	Performers Trunks
43	40	Big Top Center Poles, 62 feet long
44	35	Big Top Quarter Poles (Red)
45	31/6	Big Top Quarter Poles (Blue)
46	16	Concession Dept.
47	16	Ring Stock Trappings
48	20	Ring Stock Tent & Poles
49	16	Ring Stock Trappings & Trunks
50	16	Ring Stock Stake & Chain
51	19	Trunks
52	14	Props
53	22	Dressing Room Tent & Poles
54	21	Performing Stages
55	18	Trunks & Props
56	16	Trunks & Props
57	22	Props
58	26	Props
59	18	Trunks
60	18	Trunks
61	18	Trunks
62	18	Trunks
63	16	Props
64	16	Wardrobe
65	16	Trunks & Props
66	18	Props
67,69,70-82 84,85,87-91 93-95	16 (approx.)	25 Cages & Dens
86,96,97	16	Giraffe Wagons
100	12	Public Address System
101	17	Grease Joint
102	10/6	Water Wagon
104	10/6	Water Wagon
105	16	Layout Wagon
106,107,108	12	Stake Drivers
109	16	Menagerie Trappings
110,111,112	16	Light Plants
113,114	16	Light Plant Equipment
115,116,119,120	17	Sideshow Panel Fronts
117	16	Elephant Trappings
118	16	Band Tent & Wardrobe
121	16	Yellow Ticket Wagon
122	16	White Ticket Wagon
123	18	Red Ticket Wagon
124	16	Office
126	16	Light Plant
139	20	Seat Jacks
140,141	20	Automobile Wagons
142,143	31	Chairs
153	20	Ring Curbs & Equipment
1220	14	Train Light Plant

The loads carried by the canvas wagons would double in weight when the tents were loaded on a rainy night—from four tons to eight tons or more. The pole wagons on any circus were long and carried massive loads. On *Ringling Bros. and Barnum & Bailey* the center pole wagon was forty feet long and was loaded with seven poles, six for the big top and one spare, sixty-two feet long and weighing approximately one ton each.

Another enormous load was carried by the wagons that contained the electric light plants. The plank wagons, stringer wagons, and seat wagons also carried massive weights.

So the Percherons had their work cut out for them, rain or shine, when moving this vast array of circus vehicles on a daily basis.

As can be seen in this 1939 photo, circus wagons are big and strong. Note #23 Wagon has a body pole and two lead bars hanging on steel hooks. The Water Wagon carries a set of lead bars on a hook at the rear of the tank. *Circus World Museum, Baraboo, Wisconsin.*

Every circus had a special wagon to carry the center-poles. In this 1918 photo, the Ringling Bros. Circus is loading out for the first time in the spring at their winter-quarters in Baraboo, Wisconsin. Ten Percherons handle the load. *Jim McRoberts Collection.*

This circus painted its wagons the traditional "Ringling" red with the undercarriage white. The striping was red and blue. #18 Wagon carried reserved chairs. Its body was eight feet wide. Note that the body overhangs the wheels. Also note that a spare wheel is carried under the wagon. *Circus World Museum, Baraboo, Wisconsin.*

A wagon like this might be 40 feet long. 1936 photo. *Author's Collection.*

Once on the showgrounds, the wagons were spotted as near to the department that used their contents as possible. Note four canvas water troughs leaning against the wagon in the center. *Author's Collection.*

This wagon, with open top, is loaded with paraphernalia, its sides laden with tent poles and a "possum belly" compartment hung under the wagon for additional equipment. It is a mighty load for the team. 1937 on Ringling. *Circus World Museum, Baraboo, Wisconsin.*

#70 Wagon on Cole Bros. Circus, seen here on July 24, 1939 in Fond du Lac, Wisconsin, enroute over city streets to the showgrounds, is weighted down with poles and other equipment lashed to steel brackets. It has a drop bottom that adds eight to ten inches of interior height to the rear two-thirds of the wagon body. Note rear door configuration. The lower half hinges down to the ground, and the upper doors are hinged to open out. The wagon carries the tent and equipment for the ring stock. *Author's Photo.*

The driver is coming off the wagon while his helper is already unhooking the wheel team. A wagon like this could carry performers' trunks. The body is 17½ feet long and 7 feet wide. The height off the ground is 11 feet. The drop body adds about ten inches of head room in the interior. 1932 West Allis, Wisconsin. *Author's Photo.*

Compartments hanging below the wagon body as seen here were called "possum bellys." Note that this wagon has a small door on the side toward the front of the wagon that was probably used for carrying small tools. Ringling Show. *Author's Photo.*

Many of the big wagons were equipped with the same wheels, both as to axle size, diameter, and width. So the shows carried spare wheels suspended under some wagons that could fit many vehicles. *Author's Photo.*

THE CIRCUS BOYS ARE READY FOR A BUSY SEASON! ARE YOU?

A PHOTOGRAPH SHOWING ONE OF OUR PRODUCTS

WHEELS FOR AUTOMOBILES, TRUCKS, TRAILERS.	CIRCUS WAGON WHEELS FOR THE SEASON 1922 **ST. MARYS WHEEL & SPOKE CO.** CONSOLIDATED WITH CRANE & MacMAHON, INC. **ST. MARYS, OHIO**	HORSE DRAWN VEHICLE WHEELS. FELLOES, SPOKES, HUBS, SHAFTS.

The St. Marys Wheel and Spoke Co. was one of the largest manufacturers of circus wheels in America. They produced the massive and well-built wheels in all sizes, as seen on this piece of 1922 advertising material. *Author's Collection.*

This set of wheels, axles, axle nuts, and skeins are fresh out of the Beggs factory. All circus wheels revolved on tapered friction bearings. They always had 16 spokes and sometimes 18, as compared to 14 on farm, or commercial wagons. Spokes up to two inches in diameter were made of second-growth hickory, while larger spokes were made of second-growth white oak. The steel hubs were known as Sarven Patent design. This type of hub produced a much stronger wheel than those with a wooden hub. Wheels cost between $75 and $125 each, with $20 extra to sunburst them in 1920. The Beggs Wagon Company also manufactured baggage, cage, and parade wagons for many circuses. *J.W. Beggs Collection.*

An 18-spoke St. Marys Wheel with a Sarven Patent hub. Photo taken at the factory. *Author's Collection.*

A masssive wheel like this weighed 350 pounds. It is 37″ in diameter. The tire is 8″ wide and 1″ thick. On wheels of this size, the Krupp method of manufacture was used on the felleos. Note that they are made in eight equal curved segments. Each segment is made of four laminated pieces bolted together. The outside edge of this steel hub is 8½″ in diameter and has a 7/8″ thick wall. The spokes are oval in shape, 2″ × 3″. A wheel of this size was probably used on a Canvas Wagon or a Light Plant Wagon. *Author's Photo.*

If every day were sunny and the showgrounds were grassy and firm, circus wagons would be considered to be over-engineered. However, they were built to withstand the worst possible conditions. Note all of the iron reinforcing and massiveness of this Ringling wagon. *Author's Photo.*

Note the large nut on the threaded end of the axle. The cotter pin is inserted outside the diameter with a ¾″ thick wall. *Author's Photo.*

Cage wagons did not carry heavy loads, but they, too, sank into the soft mud or sand. They were constructed so that 30 or 40 horses would not pull them apart on a bad lot. *Barkin-Herman & Assoc.*

Bandwagon for the Pawnee Bill Wild West Show was built in 1903 by the Sebastian Wagon Works in New York City. It is 21½ feet long and 12½ feet high, and weighs 10,000 pounds empty. Seats on top between the skyboards will accommodate an 18-piece band. The cavernous interior could carry an enormous amount of baggage. *Author's Photo.*

Close-up of left front corner of the Pawnee Bill bandwagon. *Barkin-Herman & Assoc.*

A trademark for a railroad circus wagon is the corner bull ring. Without it the wagon could not be unloaded from, or loaded onto, the flatcars. These rings also serve as a place to hook onto by extra teams if the wagon is bogged in soft ground. *Author's Photo.*

A well-built baggage wagon. Note the hand-operated wheel brake and the footboard. The latter is hinged so that it can be folded down when loaded on the flatcars. This prevents it from being smashed if this #38 Wagon rolls too close to the wagon ahead of it. The railing on the roof is to hold extra baggage that is then lashed down and tied to the rings. #38 is 17'6" long, 11' high, and 7'10" wide. *Circus World Museum, Baraboo, Wisconsin.*

This fine team of Percherons on the 1921 Howes Great London Circus is waiting to be hitched to a wagon for the street parade. What is interesting in this photo is the heavy stick (or sawed-off sledgehammer handle) hanging on the hame of the off-wheeler. Once the team is hitched, the driver's assistant, who will be the brakeman, will take this stick to the top of the wagon with him. When he needs to apply the hand wheel brakes, he will put this stick through the spokes and thus gain extra leverage to tighten the brake shoes against the wheel. *William White Photo.*

#99 is an enormous wagon and carried an enormous load. The open-topped wagon carried pedestals, chain, chutes, rope, ring curbs, and other heavy props and rigging. It is 17½″ long, 11′6″ high, and weighs five tons empty. The wheels have steel tires one inch thick and eight inches wide. Note the ladder, footboard, hand-operated brakes, safety chains, corner bull rings, and drag shoe. *Circus World Museum, Baraboo, Wisconsin.*

Front running gear from Hagenbeck-Wallace #88 Wagon. The colossal strength built into these vehicles is quite obvious. The fifth wheel is 56″ in diameter, and the mighty St. Mary's wheels are 6″ wide and have a 31″ diameter. *Author's Photo.*

The wagon body extends out over the wheels, giving it an almost eight-foot width. The racks on the side carry additional equipment when the show is moving. *Circus World Museum, Baraboo, Wisconsin.*

The typical circus wagon axle is eight feet long and is made of forged steel. This one is 3½" square. Some are four inches. The tapered end from the flange on the right to the threaded end is 12". The threaded end is 2¾". The large tapered end is 3½" in diameter, and the small tapered end is 3" in diameter. The forged flange between the square axle and tapered end is 5½" in diameter and is one inch thick. The groove in the tapered end is a grease cavity. *Author's Photo.*

Wagons were either equipped with a foot brake or a hand-operated wheel-type brake, as shown here. To give the brakeman more leverage, a sledgehammer handle was frequently used on the wheel. The lightweight wagons generally had foot brakes; the heavy loaded wagons generally had hand brakes. *Circus World Musuem, Baraboo, Wisconsin.*

The Hagenbeck-Wallace Circus adopted this flop clevis to hold the wagon pole into the hound, rather than using a pin. Wagon poles like that in the photo were 12″ to 14″ wide and 3″ thick. *Author's Photo.*

A safety chain, as shown, is standard equipment. A chain like this is mounted on each side of the hound. These chains are hooked in place when the wagon is being poled on or off the flatcars. If the wheel should hit a cinder, rock, or piece of wood on the flatcar deck, the safety chains limit the whip to the pole, thus preventing injury to the poler. When not in use, these chains hang on hooks provided on the front of the wagon. *Author's Photo.*

Wagon restoration at circus winterquarters was an annual event. Here the men work on cages belonging to the Al G. Barnes Circus in their 1930 Baldwin Park, California, quarters. *Author's Collection.*

In 1939, when the Cole Bros. Circus got to the lot in Fond du Lac, Wisconsin, the right rear wheel was removed by the blacksmith for a repair job. Note the tapered axle end. The end of the axles always have left-handed threads. This causes the nut to tighten as the wagon moves forward. Note also the brake shoe. *Author's Photo.*

One of the major features in the design of any circus wagon is the ability to turn the wheels completely under the wagon body. This enabled a team to move the big wagons around tight lots and turn them practically on a dime. *Author's Photo.*

Getting ready for a parade on the Howes Great London Circus. Note that the team has the front wheels turned completely under the wagon. *Jim McRoberts Collection.*

In 1924, the Al G. Barnes Circus had their winterquarters in Culver City, California. In this photo, the overhaul work is concentrated on the running gear. *Author's Collection.*

The Beggs wagon factory in Kansas City, Missouri, turned out some fine circus wagons. A half dozen small cross cages are shown here. They were built in 1908 for Fred Buchanan's Yankee Robinson Circus. *J.W. Beggs Collection.*

In January 1923, Christy Bros. Circus ran this ad in *Billboard* magazine. Getting wagons in shape for a long, hard season ahead was crucial to a successful season. *Author's Collection.*

Some circuses were not large enough to have their own facilities and would take advantage of local wagon builders who let their services be known in *Billboard* ads like this one in November 1924. *Author's Collection.*

By 1927, the date of this ad, few wagon builders were left. An advertisement in *Billboard*, like this one, would bring in business for the winter months. *Author's Collection.*

Decorative wood caging used on the parade wagons was always especially made to order. *Billboard* ad, 1924. *Author's Collection.*

Letterhead used around 1910. It was as flashy as those used by the circuses with whom they did business. *J.W. Beggs Collection.*

A page from the 1910 Beggs Wagon Company catalog. *Author's Collection.*

Beggs Wagon Co.

MANUFACTURERS OF

CIRCUS WAGONS

Band Wagons, Ticket Wagons, Cages, Calliopes, Racing Chariots,
Tableau Wagons, Baggage Wagons, Carnival Wagons,
Gears and Wagon Parts

35—YEARS EXPERIENCE—35

—— OFFICE AND FACTORY ——
MICHIGAN AND GUINOTTE AVENUES Kansas City, Mo., U. S. A.

Beggs produced many exceptionally fine-quality circus wagons. This is a page from their 1910 catalog. *Author's Collection.*

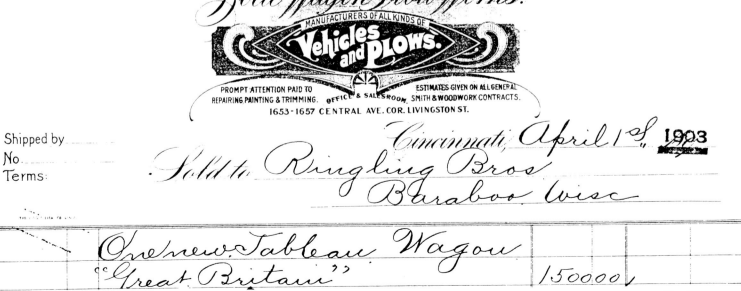

Invoice of 1903 for $1,500 to cover the cost of the Great Britain Bandwagon. This enormous vehicle is illustrated in this chapter. *Author's Collection.*

The Wagons / 93

H. L. Witt & Sons

Business
and Show

WAGONS

OF ALL KINDS
Morristown, Tennessee

Circus Cages, Dens, Calliopes
and Chariots Built to Order

All of the 1914 Cages, Dens and Vehicles
Used by Sun Brothers' Shows are from
the Factories of H. L. Witt & Sons

Any circus that did not have its own wagon shops would be anxious to know about this company that did work for Sun Bros. Circus in 1914. *Author's Collection.*

By the 1930s, the Ringling Bros. and Barnum & Bailey Circus was building their own wagons at winterquarters, because the motorized age had wiped out the commercial wagon builders. *Author's Collection.*

The Sebastian Wagon Co. of New York City specialized in show wagons of all types. In the winter of 1902-03, they produced some truly magnificent vehicles for Barnum & Bailey Circus, and also for Pawnee Bill's Wild West Show. *John Lentz Collection.*

CHAPTER 4

The Stockcars and the Runs

Mike Tschudy, Boss Hostler on the *Al G. Barnes-Sells-Floto Circus* in the 1930s, when talking about harness said, "The baggage stock was harnessed at approximately 5:30 P.M., leaving the stable at 6:00 P.M. They carried the harness until they returned to the horse tops the following morning, usually in a different city. Before being loaded into the stockcars at night, the trace chains were run through the ring in the hame and then placed over the hame. The crupper was removed from under the tails and then went over the hame. The bit was removed from the mouth and snapped under the chin, or alongside the bridle on some shows.

"The horses were then loaded either to the right or left of the center door. The loading order was never changed during the season. Horses that worked together stood together in the cars. A 72-foot stockcar loaded thirty head." (Note: fifteen horses faced one side of the car and fifteen the opposite side.)

Tschudy continues in his letter:

> The loading doors were located in the middle of the car, one on each side, so the horses could be loaded from one side but unloaded from the other in the next town, if necessary. The loading ramp hung under the car and could be pulled from either side. If the design of the railroad car prevented this arrangement then the circus had two ramps, one for each side. A manger ran down the side of the car in front of the horses. It had a lid that closed over the grain that was placed there by the watchman during the day. On top of the lids the watchman had placed hay so the horses had a bite to eat when they were loaded.

> In the early morning as the circus train neared the show town, the watchman walked along the top of the stockcars and raised the manger lids, exposing the grain to the horses. He did this by lifting a chain that ran from the hinged manger lid up a pipe to the top of the car where he hooked the chain into a notch in the pipe to hold the manger open. Thus, just before going to work, the Percherons all had a good feed of oats.

> Each horse was held in place by a short chain running from the car side to the halter. Suspended from the roof of the car over each horse's withers was a chain. This chain was run through a ring in the top of the hame strap and the collar was raised off the horse's neck slightly. This took the weight of the collar off the horse. If, through rough handling by the railroad, a horse went down, an "S" hook on this collar chain would straighten out releasing the collar; thus the horse could not choke.

> In loading, the off-wheeler of a team went in first, followed by the near wheeler. This was repeated with the body teams and leaders. A train team generally loaded in the doorway. The first horse in was turned around facing the way he entered, then the last, or wedge, horse came up the ramp and crowded his way into place. The horses were tightly loaded for a purpose. They were braced from falling if the engineer jerked the train as he took up the slack. When each team was loaded, the driver and helper could then head down the track to their sleeping car.

Some few horses required special attention, such as hobbles on rear or front legs. This prevented kicking by an ill-tempered horse. Also, a few horses got in the habit of rubbing and itching their tails on the stockcar side behind them. The driver, or helper, would bandage with canvas strips the upper part of the tail so the horse would not rub the hair off and even rub the skin raw.

The stockcars carrying horses were usually located directly behind the locomotive because there was less jolting and jerking as the engineer took up slack, or let out slack, as he picked up the cars or braked the train. On occasion, rough handling by the engineer caused serious trouble.

In 1931 when the *Hagenbeck-Wallace Circus* was on the C&O Railway going through a tunnel near Staunton, Virginia, the engineer suddenly braked the train violently. The jolt threw six draft horses off their feet. One animal was trampled to death, and a number were cut and severely bruised.

"The *Walter L. Main Circus* had a close brush with catastrophe in 1925 when on the run from Sutton, West Virginia, to Weston. A stockcar loaded with draft horses derailed while rounding a curve. Moving slowly at the time, the engineer stopped the train in time to avoid disaster. Had the derailed car listed several inches more it would have been precipitated down a mountain. The horses in the car were unloaded. The car was placed back on the rails and within an hour the train was on its way again," reported *Billboard Magazine*.

Collisions and derailments were terrifying experiences for both men and animals on railroad circuses. The circus just mentioned, *Walter L. Main*, encountered one of the most devastating wrecks in circus history in 1893 about four miles west of Tyrone, Pennsylvania. The show train was on a long downgrade with a severe curve at the bottom. The locomotive did not have the braking power to slow down the train, resulting in a total disaster. The cars derailed and slewed into a field, smashing up most of the cars, including three stockcars containing the horses. The sickening crash left 69 out of 130 horses (baggage and ring stock) dead or injured to the extent that the showmen deemed it necessary they be shot, a depressing and heart-rending situation for the Boss Hostler and his drivers.

One of the great tragedies to draft horses occurred during the 1892 season on *Ringling Bros. Circus* on May 17 while the circus train was enroute from Beloit, Kansas, to Concordia, Kansas, on the Missouri Pacific Railway. One mile east of Concordia at 2:45 A.M., a bridge undermined by high water collapsed under the first section of the circus train. Twenty-six draft horses were drowned when the cars were dumped into the river. Fourteen more drafters had torn and ripped bellies or broken legs and had to be destroyed. Ringlings immediately advertised locally for fifty horses, 1,200 to 1,600 pounds. John Ringling bought a carload of draft horses in Chicago, and on May 21 a car of twenty drafters arrived in Wichita and joined the show.

A less serious derailment for the baggage stock occurred near Zumbrota, Minnesota, on the Chicago and Great Western Railway that was hauling *Ringling Bros. and Barnum & Bailey Circus* in 1928. When the cars left the rails, one of the stockcars was split open and left dangling on top of a trestle. Two fine Percherons were thrown out and killed.

Long-string driver Ed Binner was on the *Al G. Barnes Circus*. Later, he was on the *Ringling Show* where he had an eight-up of Blue Roans in 1935. When asked about suspending the collars when the draft stock was in the cars and enroute, he remembered, "On the *Barnes Show* it was compulsory to use a chain to hang the collars. On *Ringling*, I and a few other drivers, did not do this as we thought cinders blowing in could settle on the necks and cause sores, and these were hard to heal. Some of us drivers would always check the collars after the team was unloaded to be sure no cinders were trapped in the hair under the collar. Dutch Warner, one of our long-string drivers, said he would never trust this checking to his helper. One little cinder under the collar of a working horse could cause trouble for the horse and an enormous headache and extra work for the driver."

Each day the manure was removed from the stockcars so that at night the baggage stock was standing on dry planking when they were loaded.

When the horses were unloaded in the morning they came out of the cars in the order they were made up into teams—the leaders first. Once the teams were all lined up, the helper put the bits into their mouths. They ran the checks and lines, then tied the lines on the wheel-horse hame. Then the driver mounted the near-wheeler and took the team down to the unloading crossing. Here the daily work began. The train teams on some railroad shows would pull the runs from under the wagons. The train crew would set the runs. Next the train teams (2 horses) would pull the wagons over the flatcar decks to the runs, where the vehicles would roll down to street level. These horses were called "pull-over" teams. Now a "pull-away" team of two horses took the wagon away from the unloading area. They would park it on the street where it would be picked up by the four-, six-, or eight-up team assigned to it for the haul to the showgrounds.

At night when the show was being loaded, the "pull-away" teams used in the morning were assigned new chores. They were "pull-up" teams at night, meaning they pulled the wagons up the runs onto the decks of the flatcars. The team moved alongside the flatcar during this action. If a wagon was particularly heavy, a snatch block and tackle was used to move the wagon up the runs. This cut the load the team had to pull.

Jim "Mushmouth" Traver, an eight-horse driver for *Ringling Bros.* in the early part of the century, explained the loading:

When I brought my wagon to the runs at night to be loaded, a man with a chock block stood ready to block the rear wheel of my wagon in order to stop it at the exact right spot. When the guy threw the chock, I would stop the team. Then I would swing the horses around in front of the runs. This would swing the front of the wagon around so it lined up with the runs. The chocker held his block in place so the wagon did not move forward. Now my leaders would be stepping over the foot of the runs.

When I had the wagon lined up my helper and I would get off and unhitch the wheelers from the pole and walk away. A pull-up team moved the wagon toward the runs as a poler grabbed the goose neck and kept it lined up. Now the guy with the chock walked alongside the rear wheels as the wagon went up the runs. If a rope, or chain, from the pull-up team broke, he was there with the chock to stop the backward movement of the wagon. Even if nothing broke, if the pull-up team had to suddenly stop for some crazy reason, the chocker could hold the wagon on the runs.

The width of the street where we loaded was important. If it was narrow, an eight-up with a long twenty-foot wagon had a tough time of it. But we always made out and got the show loaded.

Unexpected and sudden tragedy struck a circus occasionally. In 1931 when a circus was loading on the B&O Railway, an express train thundered along a row of boxcars and smashed into an eight-horse team on the street. Five horses were killed. Three broke away and escaped injury, as did the driver.

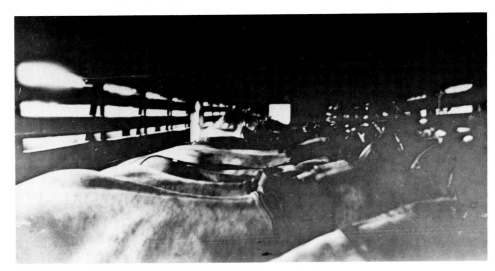

A rare photo of the inside of a loaded stockcar. The draft horses at the photographer's end of the car all face to the right. The horses in the far end all face to the left. This photo was taken in 1925 on the Ringling Show. *Frank Updegrove Photo.*

A baggage horse comes down the ramp carefully. This ramp is carried in steel brackets slung under the car. Ringling Bros. Circus, 1918, at Memphis. *Jim McRoberts Collection.*

Cole Bros. Circus baggage stock unloading in Cincinnati in 1940. As the horses came out of the cars, they were made up into their teams. *Harold Gorsuch Photo.*

This 1924 scene on the Al G. Barnes Circus shows a nice array of grade Percherons. It is interesting to note that all the horses have their bridles removed and hanging on the hames. *Author's Collection.*

Pawnee Bill's Wild West Show unloads draft stock in 1905. The wheeler walks down the ramp unattended to the driver's outstretched arm. John Van Matre Collection.

A helper gives this horse a steadying hand by grabbing its tail. Perhaps as the tail slipped through his fingers, this gesture kept the horse from stepping off the side of the ramp. Ringling Bros. Circus in 1912 in Menominee, Michigan. Ben Fernstrum Photo.

In the 1920s, Christy Bros. Circus bragged about their superior horses. Jim McRoberts Collection.

As the horses came out of the cars, they lined up in team formation—leaders, as seen here, then body pole teams, and finally wheelers. Cole Bros. Circus, 1940, in Cincinnati. Harold Gorsuch Photo.

Joe Wallace on horseback is Cole Bros. Circus Boss Hostler. Here, in 1940 in Cincinnati, he is giving orders to the drivers before they start for the runs to pick up wagons. *Harold Gorsuch Photo.*

Sells-Floto stockcars in 1918 were painted with red lettering. In this Horton, Kansas, view, the baggage stock is awaiting orders. *Jules Bourguin Photo.*

The six- and eight-horse teams are lined up along the railroad tracks. Soon they will move to pick up a wagon to haul to the showgrounds. RBB&B, 1925. *Frank Updegrove Photo.*

In this 1938 scene on Ringling Bros. and Barnum & Bailey Circus at Buffalo, New York, the drafters are coming from the stockcars and are awaiting the wagons that will soon hit the street. *Jerry Booker Photo.*

When loaded into the stockcars with their rumps up against a plank on the wall, a horse would occasionally get into the habit of rubbing his tail on the plank. This horse was given a canvas sack, as seen here, so that he would not rub the hair off, or worse, rub the skin raw. Ringling Bros. Circus, 1915. *Author's Collection.*

A six-up moves along the bricks to the runs. Note that the traces are still hooked to the hames. *Circus World Museum, Baraboo, Wisconsin.*

In this 1914 scene, the draft horses of the Hagenbeck-Wallace Circus have just been unloaded. The two-horse teams headed this way appear to be train teams going down to the runs to begin the task of unloading wagons. *Author's Collection.*

When the big railroad circuses arrived in town, the red wagons had to be unloaded and hauled to the showgrounds. Percheron power did the job. In this photo, men are readying the runs down which the wagons will roll. *Gene Baxter Photo.*

In 1928, the Christy Bros. Circus just did not have horses—they had prize Belgians and Percherons. This is one more bit of flash that added to the overall excitement of the circus coming to town. The second car in line is lettered "Dancing Horses." *Gene Baxter Collection.*

Albany, New York, 1930. The big show has arrived from Utica on the New York Central Railroad. The runs are set. Wagon #65 will be brought down to the street, at which time one of the two teams shown will pull it down the street and out of the way. *Gene Baxter Photo.*

The grey team has stopped and will turn and go back along the flats to get another wagon. RBB&B, 1936, at New Bedford, Massachusetts. *Ed Tracy Photo.*

The "pullover" team on the right has finished its job once the wagon starts rolling down the runs. A man controlling a snubbing rope attached to the rear bull ring on the wagon brakes the wagon on the runs and stops it when it is on the ground. *Author's Photo.*

The pullover teams learn quickly to straddle the rails and to step nimbly over them. This team on the Al G. Barnes Circus in 1931 is unloading the big wagons at Alhambra, California. *Author's Collection.*

Wagon #66 is moving over the crossover plates set between the flats. The Percherons walk steadily along in this 1936 scene at New Bedford, Massachusetts. Note the rope man—he will unhook his rope from the wagon when it starts rolling down the runs. The team, driver, and rope man will swing around and go back along the flats for another wagon. *Ed Tracy Photo.*

The team on the left is turning around to go back down the tracks to pick up another wagon. The big wagon is being guided down the runs by the poler. When the wagon is on the street, the team on the right will haul it out of the way, where an eight-horse team will hitch on and take it to the lot. Al G. Barnes Circus, 1935. *Jim McRoberts Collection.*

An excellent view of the runs. The black Percherons are the pullover team in this scene. As the wagons hit the street, one of the long-string teams waiting will take it to the lot. Sparks Circus unlaoding at Barrie, Ontario, in 1928. *Jim McRoberts Collection.*

Congestion on the streets of Erie, Pennsylvania, in 1940, when Cole Bros. Circus was unloading. The two-train teams stand along the flats. An 8-up is approaching and will take one of these first wagons off to the lot. *Jerry Booker Photo.*

At Beatrice, Nebraska, in 1936, this team of Percherons moves a massive load across the flats. Each of the seven center poles weighs a ton and are 62' long. The total load is approximately ten tons.

The pull-away team of dapple greys get #60 Wagon out of the way. This wagon is carrying a particularly heavy load—note that it is equipped with a double set of brake shoes, both in front and behind the rear wheel. Also note the spare wheel slung under the body. 1938 at Milwaukee. *Author's Photo.*

Two pullover teams were put to work on this wagon on the Al G. Barnes Circus. *W. F. Tschudy Collection.*

The dapple greys are moving the wagon foreward. The poler is holding the wheels in line. On the immediate left of the wagon can be seen the snubber, who will brake the wagon as it rolls free down the runs. The man with the chock block in the street will stop the wagon in an emergency. Cole Bros. Circus in 1939, Fond du Lac, Wisconsin. *Author's Photo.*

This excellent team of Percherons moves a heavily loaded stringer wagon. The pull-away team will park the wagon down the street and out of the way. Al G. Barnes-Sells Floto Circus, 1937. *W.F. Tshchudy Collection.*

A very good view of the pull-away team. Note that the lead bars are equipped with a chain that has a hook. The hook is fastened to the gooseneck on the wagon pole. The wagon on the runs is held there by the snubber until #85 Wagon is moved out. 1938 at Milwaukee. *Author's Photo.*

#80 is on the street, and this pull-away team of Percherons scratches and slips on bricks and rails to move the load down the street. Hagenbeck-Wallace Circus at Buffalo, New York, 1938. *Jerry Booker Photo.*

The lead bars for this pull-away team are of a different style. Note that the chain is missing. There is a handle on the lead bar so the rigging can be lifted up and the ring slipped over the gooseneck. This arrangement, about 1930, does not show up in many photos. Perhaps it was too clumsy. *John Zweifel Collection.*

On the far left side of the photo is a 6-up waiting for #61 Wagon, which the grey team is delivering. Beyond the greys is a team of roans coming back for another wagon. The citizens of Fond du Lac, Wisconsin, enjoyed this unusual performance as Cole Bros. Circus unloaded July 24, 1939. *Author's Photo*.

When the show loaded, the operation was as smooth and efficient as when unloading. The drafters on the left are now acting as a pull-up team to pull the cage wagon up the runs. *W.F. Tschudy Collection.*

Ringling Bros. and Barnum & Bailey Circus set up their canvas water troughs near the unloading area so that their teams could get a cool drink. 1925. *Frank Updegrove Photo.*

Loading the Percherons was quick and easy. Their traces were looped and hung on the hames. The bit was removed from the horse's mouth and snapped alongside the bridle, and cruppers on the wheel horses were removed and hung on the hames. Once loaded, a chain suspended from the railroad car ceiling held this load of harnesses slightly off the horeses's neck. RBB&B, 1925. *Frank Updegrove Photo.*

Before rolling the stockcar door shut, a heavy plank is slipped in place behind the drafters. Hagenbeck-Wallace Circus, 1915. *Author's Collection.*

This is Ringling Bros. Circus around 1916. There are unanswered questions here. Why are the draft horses being loaded without harness? Where was the harness carried? Note in this photo that the storage location for the ramp is clearly seen. It is carried across the tie rods. *Steve Albasing Photo.*

The devastating train wreck of the Walter L. Main Circus in 1893 near Tyrone, Pennsylvania. The entire train roared downhill out of control and slewed off the track on a sweeping curve. All cars, including three stockcars, were demolished. Sixty-nine of one hundred thirty horses were killed or had to be destroyed. Many of the noble drafters are seen here as they fell. *Author's Collection*.

In 1924, the last show town of the season was Greensboro, North Carolina, for Ringling Bros. and Barnum & Bailey Circus. Seen here are the draft stock waiting for the word to load for the trip to winterquarters in Bridgeport, Connecticut. *Frank Updegrove Photo*.

In 1924 on the long haul at the end of the season from the last showtown, Greensboro, North Carolina, to winterquarters in Bridgeport, Connecticut, the Ringling Circus stopped enroute. These were called feed and water stops. The draft stock was unloaded, exercised, fed hay and watered. This must have been a startling sight for the towers to suddenly see 350 or more Percherons. *Frank Updegrove Photo*.

CHAPTER 5

To and From the Lot

Usually each long-string team made two trips in the morning hauling wagons from the unloading area to the lot. The teams were generally assigned to the same loads in the morning and again in the evening.

The circuses played one-day stands, except for a few big cities on the season's route. Each town presented a different situation. Some had their circus showgrounds three or four miles from the railroad yards. When *Ringling* played Milwaukee's lake front, the situation was the opposite. The unloading track adjoined the lot, thus wagons jammed up while waiting to be spotted. The circus wagons and animals trouping through residential districts put on quite an unusual show for the towners along the route between the showgrounds and the railroad yards.

Both in the morning on the way to the lot and at night on the way to the runs, the drivers followed the torches that marked out the route. These kerosene torches, or flares, were set on the curbs at intersections. For example, as a team approached an intersection if the torch was on the right-hand corner curb, this told the driver to make a right turn. If it was on the left corner curb he made a left turn. If the torch was on the right corner curb across the intersection this meant he was to go straight ahead. Frequently, the morning route was different than the evening route, due to the fact the circus would arrive in town on one railroad, but pull out of town on a different railroad. During the day the cars were switched to a new location, perhaps a mile away crosstown. The flare wagon was the last to leave the lot in the evening. A man assigned to this vehicle had the job of picking up all the flares along the route.

Many a city the circuses played had some steep hills that had to be navigated either to or from the railroad yards, or in parade. The lightweight wagons were equipped with a foot brake; the heavy vehicles, as a rule, had hand brakes that were equipped with a wheel to wind up the chain, thus clamping the brake shoe against the wheel. In addition, every wagon had a drag shoe* hanging on the underside in front of the left rear wheel.

If, while enroute, a steep downhill grade had to be navigated, two blacksmith's helpers were stationed at the top of the hill. When a team came along, the driver would stop the horses. The blacksmith's helpers would unhook the drag shoe and place it on the pavement in front of the wheel. The driver then rolled the wagon forward onto the drag shoe, which was securely fastened to the wagon body by a heavy chain. Thus, the left rear wheel would skid down the incline.

---

*In the era of circus history that we are concerned with in this book, every wagon was equipped with a drag shoe. The reason this piece of equipment is being discussed in this chapter, rather than in *Chapter 3* on *Wagons*, is that the use of the drag shoe deals with moving the circus wagons to and from the showgrounds over city streets.

At the bottom of the hill two more blacksmith's helpers would be ready to remove the drag shoe. When the wagon stopped, the chain between the drag shoe and wagon body would be as taut as a violin string. However, there was a release lock called a "let-go-quick" in this chain, so designed that when a steel ring was hit, the ring would slide forward, thus releasing a hook that jumped open, dropping the chain to the pavement. The driver then moved the wagon forward a few feet, the wheel rolling over the drag shoe and onto the pavement. The shoe would then be picked up and hung back on the wagon.

In some cities where the hills were severe and the brick pavement was slick, the circus men sanded the street to give the drag shoe something to grip onto. The drag shoe functioned not only on the baggage wagons going to and from the lot, but occasionally the street parade had to navigate a steep hill. In some cities there was no way to avoid such a hill, so the drag shoe was put into play.

This operation on hills did not always go smoothly. Let Irvine Hetherington, long-string driver, tell in his own words about three such episodes:

I was helping "Apples" Welsh at the time and Nick Strauss, a split-eight driver, made the trip down for Apples as Apples wasn't feeling well, on the stable pole wagon. We attempted to hold that wagon with a brake, but it didn't work. We did not use the drag shoe. If it was nowadays we would have killed people, but it was a very snappy eight, and when I hollered at Nick and he saw the wagon was getting the best of him, he yelled at Prince and Barney, the leaders, and went down that hill on a gallop, never hurt anyone. We had a blind horse on the near-four horse body named Peggy, and she kept her feet. When we got to the bottom of the hill, we slowed to a trot and Ed Farley, the old train watch, when we came around the corner on the trot, said the fire was right over there.

That same team, the year after, Welsh was driving them and he was coming down the hill in Kansas City with a Hippo Den, a very heavy wagon, and it had a boxcar brake on it. When it started to get away, Welsh hollered to the brakeman to wind it up. He said he had it as tight as he could get it. He was a fellow, short and a large head, an Englishman, and on account he knew more than anyone else did, he had the nickname of "Shorty Knowall." His

right name was Ed. J. Sharp. Then Welsh hollered to him to wind it the other way, but by the time he got it the other way, two horses were down and were killed. The wheelers, Hutch and Austin, were dragged. They were sent back to winter quarters and did not do anymore work that year.

Hetherington continued his letter:

Later, I don't know when, Shorty was driving a four-horse team on the Chandelier Wagon, and he was at the top of a short hill that had a bridge at the bottom and on the other side of the bridge was a washout. An eight-horse driver named Hafey came along with a heavy wagon and said to Shorty that they don't need the Chandelier Wagon down there now but they do need this, better let me go first. Shorty said he got here first and he was going down first. He went down pretty fast and hit that washout, threw him off the seat and fell on the hips of the off-wheeler, and a wagon wheel ran over his head. Hafey told me he saw his brains fly and hit a tree. He told me if I had gone down it without a drag shoe, like he did, there would not be a grease spot left of me.

In 1909 *Ringling Bros.* opened their season in the old Madison Square Garden. After this run, the circus was scheduled to show in Brooklyn under canvas. Rather than load the show on the trains, the entire circus was gillied across town to the Brooklyn lot. Jim Traver, who was driving an eight-horse hitched on a heavy wagon, remembers the confusion and traffic snarls that resulted from this move. At one point, when he was halfway over the Brooklyn Bridge, a streetcar caught up to him, the motorman started to clang away on the bell. Traver, with his massive load, was helpless and could only keep his team moving ahead. At this point, a mounted policeman came up, sized up the situation and shouted, "Stay where you are—let that fool clang his bell."

In 1911 on the *Ringling Bros. Circus,* Jack McCracken said, "I was taking my wagon from the lot to the train. I was easing down a rather steep hill when the brake chain snapped. The wagon rolled up against the wheelers and started the team to running. The helper jumped off. The team galloped down the hill and piled up against the side of a streetcar. The two leaders were killed. I landed on the lead bars ahead of the wheelers. I broke an arm and three ribs and got skinned up badly from the horses hooves."

The *Billboard Magazine* occasionally reported problems: Bluefield, West Virginia, 1925—*Walter L. Main Circus:* "On May 1st a safety chain broke on a drag shoe on a baggage wagon while descending a hill, pushing the wagon onto one of the wheelers injuring it so badly it had to be killed." Morgantown, West Virginia, 1926—*Christy Bros. Circus:* "On returning from the parade the drag shoe slipped from under the wheel on the steam calliope and just missed causing it to go over a steep embankment, a drop of 150 feet, to the M&K tracks." Greensburg, Pennsylvania, 1934—*Hagenbeck-Wallace Circus:* "Hardest parade of the season. It was necessary to shoe all wagons on two separate hills. However, there were no mishaps."

In the early morning hours there wasn't much traffic to contend with as #92 Pole Wagon on the 1936 Al G. Barnes Circus traversed the streets between runs and lot. Note that all eight horses are sharing the load, as the body poles are all in the air. The helper walks alongside the team, probably worrying about an upcoming intersection. *Author's Collection.*

Enroute to the showgrounds in 1936, this team of eight grade Percherons takes its heavily loaded wagon through town. Al G. Barnes Circus. *Author's Collection.*

Eight roans move a heavy stringer wagon down a residential street to the showgrounds. RBB&B, 1936, in Topeka. *Jim McRoberts Photo.*

On May 9, 1912, the Mighty Haag Show played Wilmington, Ohio. Here one of their eight-hrose teams takes a wagon to the showgrounds. The fourteen-spoked, wood-hubbed wheels are rather unusual. *M.W. Organ Photo.*

In Topeka, Kansas, 1936, this Ringling 8-up are pulling their share of a big load of grandstand stringers and jacks. This wagon is 32'6" long. *Jim McRoberts Photo.*

Eight Belgians move this thirty-foot wagon through the streets of Brooklyn. Passing the team is a big Mack truck hauling canvasas and a load of workers and pulling a wagon. Hindsight tells us that as this Mack sped down the street, it was the death knell for the draft stock. Two years later Ringling sold all their baggage horses. *Circus World Museum, Baraboo, Wisconsin.*

These eight roan Belgians are beginning to make the right-angle turn. The driver, Ed Binner, is just pulling on the lines in his left hand and the leaders are responding. Note that the helper and driver are both applying pressure on the foot brake. This photo was taken in 1936 when the Ringling Show was in Newark, New Jersey. *Circus World Museum, Baraboo, Wisconsin.*

The show is Ringling Bros. and Barnum & Bailey in the 1920s. The town is unknown, but the problem is obvious—a steep hill must be navigated between the railroad unloading area at the showgrounds. The 6-up on the wagon is assisted by Shorty Stees and his 8-up. Note the team of eight on the far enbankment going down to assist with another wagon. In the distance the road is cluttered with wagons waiting to be moved. *John Zweifel Collection.*

Another view of the Big Show's peculiar problem on the way to the lot. Here Dick Sells and his eight greys are coming up the grade at a smart pace. *John Zweifel Collection.*

In 1938, when Robbins Bros. Circus was in Allentown, Pennsylvania, the show was confronted with an unusual problem of a steep hill enroute to the showgrounds. A six-horse hook rope team was stationed at the bottom of the hill, where it could assist any team with a heavy wagon, as seen here. *Robert D. Good Photo.*

Very late in the afternoon, or early evening, the trek from the showgrounds to the railroad yards begins. Note the circus tents in the background on the left. The last meal of the day has been served, and the cookhouse, no longer needed, is taken down and packed into the wagons. Once loaded, these vehicles are hauled to the runs. Here #1 Wagon, carrying a load of cookhouse tables, is hauled down the street by a very fine team of Percherons. *Circus World Museum, Baraboo, Wisconsin.*

Every circus wagon in the draft horse era carried a drag shoe, either like this one or one of very similar design. It was hung on the underside of the wagon body in front of the left rear wheel. When in use, the wheel would skid, thus acting as additional braking power on a steep downgrade. This device was occasionally required when the wagons were moving to and from the show-grounds and railroad yards and also in parades. *Author's Photo.*

A typical drag shoe showing how and where it was carried on the wagon. *Circus World Museum, Baraboo, Wisconsin.*

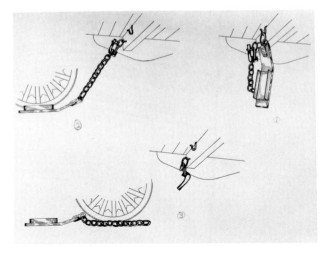

This is how the drag shoe works. #1 drawing shows it suspended from a hook under the Wagon. #2 drawing shows the shoe under the wheel. The wheel now will skid, adding materially to the ability of the driver and brakeman to get the wagon and team down a steep grade. On a six- or eight-horse hitch, only the wheel team can help hold back the wagon. The teams out front are loosely connected. Drawing #3—when the wagon has reached the bottom of the hill, an assistant hits the ring on the "let-go-quick." This causes the hook to drop, releasing the chain on the drag shoe. The wagon is then pulled forward over the shoe and is replaced on the hook under the wagon. *Walter Strong Drawing.*

Occasionally, a circus found no way to eliminate a steep hill on a street parade route. Seen here is the Hagenbeck-Wallace Circus in Vicksburg, Mississippi in 1934 using a drop shoe on their steam calliope. The dragging shoe is kicking up dust from the sand that has been spread on the slippery pavement. Note that even though the wagon is moving downhill, all six horses are pulling hard on the lot. *Joe Heiser Photo.*

As #6 Baggage Wagon on the 1922 John Robinson Circus moves downhill, the helper tightens the brakes. This action stretches out the team, requiring all six Percherons to pull the heavily loaded wagon. Note that the body pole and the doubletrees are all in the air. *Dick & Peg Hemphill Collection.*

CHAPTER 6

On the Lot

All of the various tents and departments on a circus showground are, as a rule, located in relation to the Big Top where the performance is given. Therefore, every department is located in about the same place every day, but in a different city or town. No two circus lots were the same size or shape; thus, when the show was forced to set up on a small area (circus men refer to it as a "tight lot") or one of irregular shape, exceptions to the rule immediately took place on how everything fitted together.

Ringling Bros. and Barnum & Bailey Circus, travelling on 90 to 100 railroad cars, required a ten- to twelve-acre field to set up their tents. Smaller shows, travelling on 30 railroad cars, of course, could set up on less acreage.

All of this preliminary explanation is by way of introduction to the long-string driver arriving at the showgrounds with a load. These seasoned men could quickly size up the situation. Each driver knew what equipment was in his wagon. He knew, generally, where it should be spotted. If there were any variations, the Boss Hostler or one of his assistants, all mounted, would direct the driver exactly where to go with the wagon. Once on the lot with their loads, a few four-horse teams were assigned to stake drivers. After laying out the lot, the first job to get done was pounding tent stakes into the ground. These five-foot-long pointed stakes varied from four to five inches in diameter at the steel banded top.

Teams on the pole wagons hauled their loads to the spot directed by a hostler. One pole was removed, then the team took the wagon forward. One blast of a whistle stopped the team and another pole was unloaded. Two blasts on the whistle and the pole wagon moved forward again until all poles were on the ground. Then the teams pulling wagons loaded with bales of canvas arrived and were unloaded at the designated locations. Light plant wagons were spotted around the perimeter of the big tent.

Some horses were assigned to raising center poles, raising the canvas, or setting quarter poles. When the tents were in the air and guyed out, in came the six-horse teams with the wagons holding the stringers, jacks, planks, and chairs for the seats. Other teams brought in wagons with props and rigging. It appeared to be bedlam, but in reality, it was a well-organized bunch of men and horses that knew exactly what they were doing. When the menagerie tent was in the air, the horses would pull in the cages and dens of wild animals, lining them up around the perimeter of the tent.

Some horses were assigned to water wagons as two- or four-horse teams. They got their loads at a city fire hydrant, then took the water to the cookhouse, performers tent, elephant department, or horse tents. In the case of very dusty lots, they were put on sprinkling duty.

After a driver unhooked his team from his wagon, he would neatly loop up the lines and hang them on the hame of the near-wheeler. It was this horse that he rode to his next assignment.

As these jobs were accomplished, the Percherons were sent to the Horse Tops (stable) for a rest, a feed, and a grooming.

Every circus had a harness maker. He was a busy man, keeping all the harness in perfect condition. The draft horse harness was exposed to severe strain and wear and tear. Each driver and his helper was charged with checking over the harness used by their team. If a strap or buckle needed to be replaced, it was their responsibility to take it to the harness maker for repairs.

E.L. "Spike" Hansen, who for years worked for the *Ringling Circus* and others, recalled a couple of harness makers he knew:

> With reference to the harness makers on circuses: Naturally I will first mention "Blind Waxy" Louis A. Panzer of *RB & BB*, as I saw him daily, and his helpers, as they ate at the Boss' table in the cookhouse. He had 350 sets of draft harness, plus ring stock, elephant, and miscellaneous trappings to maintain, by far more than any other circus of that period. The fact that the *Ringling Show* was able to replenish and replace worn harness, no doubt, served to lessen the repair work for the shop.
>
> I had an old horse, Plato, in the body team who never laid down at night. When the stock remained in the stables at night, Plato slept standing with halter chain stretched taut, probably to maintain better balance. Result—he often broke his halter, and he would awake staggering to keep from falling. Since we slept behind our team when not enroute, I was sure to wake as he stumbled back toward my bed. So I often made a trip to Waxey for repair of the broken halter. He seemed to know who the culprit was as he would cuss and say, "well that damn Plato broke it again."
>
> Panzer had been *Ringling's* chief harness maker for over three decades. He had been handicapped with blindness for many years, but this obstacle did not interfere with his skill and ability to do his job.

Another harness maker I knew and used to visit with was W.A. "Waxy" Dyke when he was on the *Cole Show*. Later he came over to the *Ringling Show*. He was out of Waukesha, Wisconsin, as I recall, and had been on *Al G. Barnes* and I think other corporation shows. Of course, when baggage stock was discontinued, harness repair work was considerably lessened. Waxy was a skilled workman and made an eight-horse set of harness in quarters for the *Cole Show* that was later used on their train teams. Beautiful work, nickel finish hames and spots, the leather edged with green trim. Incidently, the only time I ever saw a four-horse pull-up train team hitched tandem, termed I believe the "Gilligan or Artillery Hitch," was on *Cole Bros.*, each team wearing the harness I described. "Two-Gun Whitey" H.C. Warren was then Trainmaster.

Another harness maker I came to know in later years was "Coke Whitey" George Warner on *RB & BB*. He succeeded Dyke and I believe was the last full-time employee in that capacity on their show. In later years one of the ringstock grooms, Roy Van Denplas, did that repair work. He had been a helper to Coke Whitey in quarters and picked up his knowledge from him.

Every circus carried blacksmiths and horseshoers. The size of this crew was determined by the number of wagons and horses on the show. And the farriers were good. They had to be. Without their abilities, the show, which generally moved to a different town every day, would soon bog down.

The big problem that they faced was the fact that the horses they kept shod worked on a great variety of surfaces. In the railroad yards there were ties and rails and cinders. Between the unloading area and the showgrounds, the multiple horse hitches were moving massive wagons over streets paved with brick, sometimes with creosote blocks, or, perhaps, macadam or concrete, and in some cases paved not at all.

At the showgrounds, conditions could vary from grass to a cut hayfield that were ideal, to a filled-in dumping grounds, which was rough on horses, men, and equipment. Then, too, the surface might be sandy or stony. So the Percherons had to be well shod with shoes that were fitted right and that were on tight. With this kind of protection, the horses could set their feet firmly and use all their strength when the going was rough and tough.

As the drivers arrive on the showgrounds with their loads, they generally know about where to spot the wagon. If a special problem occurs, the Boss Hostler, or one of his assistants, will direct the driver. Here Mike Tschudy, Boss Hostler of the Al G. Barnes-Sells-Floto Combined Circus points out where he wants 110 Wagon. If this is a new man on the show this, too, would be cause for hostler directing him. Note the off-wheel horse has a cloth over its neck. This keeps flies off some kind of a minor cut or bruise. 1938. *Joe Fleming Photo.*

A 6-up of sorrel Belgians brings a cage onto the lot. The helper is handling the brake if needed. 1938 at Madison, Wisconsin. *Author's Photo.*

#40 Wagon carried side poles and some rigging. The crew in the 18-foot long wagon are unloading equipment. The team of six Percherons will follow the perimeter of the tent as the crew drops the side poles. Milwaukee 1935. *Author's Photo.*

As these two four-horse teams of black Percherons pull their cage wagons onto the lot in Madison, Wisconsin, the leaders have ears erect watching the activity ahead. 1938. *Author's Photo.*

An excellent view of the rigging on an eight-horse team. The philosophy of the circus men was not to make the horses carry the weight of the body poles and lead bars on their necks. Therefore, they used very long breast straps and neck chains. As one studies the photos of the six- and eight-horse teams in this book you will note the body poles dragging on the pavement. Rarely, if ever, did the nimble horses tangle in their rigging. Ringling Circus 1935 in Milwaukee. *Author's Photo.*

The driver on one side, and the helper on the other, are unhooking this team of grade Belgians from the heavy wagon at Milwaukee's lakefront showgrounds in 1935. The unloading area adjoined the lot so there was a congestion of wagons. They arrived before they could be spotted in their final location. *Author's Photo.*

All eight Percherons are pulling the weighty wagon onto the circus lot at Madison, Wisconsin in 1938. *Author's Photo.*

The driver is waiting for instructions. The horses stand quietly on this Madison, Wisconsin, lot in 1938 where the Al G. Barnes-Sells-Floto Circus was playing. Circus drivers, when referring to their hitches, would talk about "body pole" teams, not "swing" teams. On this 8-up, for example, there would be wheelers, four-horse body pole team, six-horse body pole teams, and the leaders. *Author's Photo.*

A hard pull across the grass. This wagon carries one of the big, electric light plants. 1938 scene at Madison, Wisconsin, on the Al G. Barnes-Sells-Floto Circus. *Author's Photo.*

Ed Binner driving his eight roans at a smart pace as they came on to the showgrounds. Red Finn is the Boss Hostler and on horseback on other side of team. Ed said, "They were a real to ahead tight line team." *Joe Fleming Photo.*

This is a very good view of the body pole and neck chains. Photo taken in Dayton, Ohio, on the Ringling Show in 1938. *Harold Gorsuch Photo.*

Eight well-matched sorrel Belgians in 1930. *Circus World Museum, Baraboo, Wisconsin.*

Eight fine matched bays on a ponderous canvas wagon in 1938 at Dayton, Ohio. *Harold Gorsuch Photo.*

The body poles all in a straight line with the wagon pole gives this load the full power of the eight Percherons. Al G. Barnes-Sells-Floto Circus at Madison, Wisconsin in 1938. *Author's Photo.*

It is rather unusual for a draft team to move along at this pace. The leaders have broken into a gallop moving this wagon the Great Wallace Circus, 1905. *Jim McRoberts Collection.*

1940 scene at Middletown, Ohio. Ted White is the driver of the chain team that is spotting the wagon. This was the last season for draft horses on this or any other circus. Trucks and tractors took over, except for a few isolated uses of Percherons as train teams in the 1940s. *Harold Gorsuch Photo.*

The blacks are bringing this cage across the lot. Hanging on the hame of the off-wheeler is a heavy stick which would be used as extra leverage on the hand brake wheel if a bad hill was on the route. 1938. *Joe Fleming Photo.*

A 6-up of greys well lined up and all pulling evenly, move a wagon across the Erie, Pennsylvania, lot in 1939 on Cole Bros. Circus. *Jerry Booker Photo.*

The circus carried these portable canvas water troughs. They were set up, generally, at the unloading area but mainly on or near the lot. If a fire hydrant was not convenient a circus water wagon kept them filled. Ringling Bros. and Barnum & Bailey 1920s. *Gene Baxter Collection.*

A first rate team of Percherons move this Ringling stake driver around the perimeter of the big tent. One blast of a whistle and the driver stops while the stakes are pounded into the ground. Two blasts on the crew foreman's whistle and the driver moves the team up. 1938 at Madison, Wisconsin. *Author's Photo.*

Another task for a team is raising the 62-foot long center poles. The rope from the team goes back to the base of the upright pole through a pulley block then up to the top of the pole, through another pulley block and over to the top of the pole being raised. This is Ringling Bros. Circus, 1915. *Author's Collection.*

This team is beginning the operation of raising the canvas tent up the center poles. This is done through an ingenious series of pulley blocks. RBB&B, 1925. *Frank Updegrove Photo.*

The daily tasks are done and this 8-up heads for the horse tent and food, rest, and a grooming. RBB&B 1924 in Cleveland, Ohio. *Frank Updegrove Photo.*

As the tent is being raised in stages by teams on the outside, teams on the underside set the quarter poles. This, too, is done by stages. RBB&B 1936 in Brooklyn, New York. *Circus World Museum, Baraboo, Wisconsin.*

Billy, an exceptional Percheron chunk, was assigned to the one-horse tent stake wagon, driven by Jim Peffers. Their task was to deliver extra stakes where needed and collect stakes that might be laying around the lot. 1937 in Milwaukee. *Author's Photo.*

One can assume the water tank is full from the way blacks are digging in. RBB&B 1925. *Frank Updegrove Photo.*

The team stands quietly while water is drawn off for the menagerie in the background. 1935. *Author's Photo.*

Water wagon duty is assigned to different teams on different days. This driver is filling his tank in West Allis, Wisconsin, showgrounds. *Author's Photo.*

Eight dapple greys head across the circus lot "travelling light." Having delivered one wagon to the showgrounds, the 8-up driver is probably heading for the street and to the runs for his second wagon. Note the hames being used as coat racks. Between the time the driver and his helper left their coach and their arrival at the horse top, the hame was the only place they could carry their rain gear, or an extra coat. Cole Bros., Erie, Pennsylvania 1939. *Jerry Booker Photo.*

An unusual assignment for the Ringling Bros. and Barnum & Bailey baggage stock in 1925. The show was set up in Grant Park, Chicago, for a ten-day stand. The problem of manure disposal was solved by hauling it to the railroad yards and dumping into gondolas provided by the Illinois Central. *Frank Updegrove Photo.*

Great activity on a tight lot. In 1933 Ringling Bros. and Barnum & Bailey Circus played Baraboo, Wisconsin, at the fairgrounds. In the distance, the huge 6-pole big top is beginning to take shape. In a couple of hours all will be in readiness for the throngs who will witness the matinee performance. The baggage stock will be munching sweet timothy hay in their tent stables. *Jim McRoberts Collection.*

By noon, ususally, the show is on the lot and set up. A tented city, the newspaper reporters used to call it. On the far left behind the banner line, one corner of the sideshow tent can be seen. On the left is the menagerie and to the right of it stretches the big top which, in this era of 1929, could seat 10,000 or more. In the left foreground can be seen light plant wagons and various small tents that function as headquarters for departments, or possibly dressing rooms for star performers. In right foreground is the dressing room tent. In the right background are horse tops. The cookhouse tents and others are out of the photo. Over 50 baggage wagons can be seen spotted around the lot. At 2:15 the matinee will begin. *Gene Baxter Collection.*

Cole Bros. harness maker Bill "Waxey" Dyke and his tools, which will include harness needles, stitching awls, creasers, ticklers, a revolving punch, saddlers pincers, claw tools, rein trimmer, saddlers hammer, round knives, trimming knife, prick punches, round punches, and many others. Dyke's idea of a good harness was one of great durability which meant quality. To produce such a harness took time. Whenever Dyke was pushed by a department boss for the job he was working on, his favorite expression was "This takes time—you don't shoot that out of a pistol." *Harold Gorsuch Photo*

Every major circus had to have a harnessmaker. These men ususally were under the direction of the Boss Hostler. Here the harness maker sits on his "stitching horse" clamping a back pad on which he is sewing a felt backing. *Circus World Museum, Baraboo, Wisconsin.*

View of the Blacksmith Shop wagon on the 1916 Barnum & Bailey Show. Like any good farrier, the horseshoer's tool box would probably contain a hoof rasp, hoof knife, claw and driving hammer, hoof nippers, hoof chisel, clinching block, nail nippers, clinch cutter and punch tool, shoe puller and large pincers. *Ringling Museum of the Cirucs*.

The blacksmiths and the horsehoers (wearing their muleskin aprons) pose for their photo in Reading, Pennsylvania, June 3, 1938. This formidable crew handled the work in Ringling Bros. and Barnum & Bailey Circus. *Ringling Museum of the Circus.*

In this 1925 scene on the Ringling Show one of the farriers takes care of a problem out on the lot. The leader either is having a loose shoe fixed, or a thrown shoe replaced. The team can then continue their assigned tasks. When the team is finally stabled, this horse will be brought to the blacksmith tent to have the job checked for permanence. *Frank Updegrove Photo.*

The blacksmith shop on the Ringling Show was operating without a tent this day, probably due to a late arrival in town. The wagon in the background carries all the equipment. Note the three forges on the right. Associated equipment and tools are anvils, pritchels, tongs, hardies, hammers, and others. *Frank Updegrove Photo.*

Each circus had one or more horshoers, depending on the number of head with the show. These farriers were experts, as nothing will cause a horse to go lame faster than a loose shoe, or one put on improperly. Cole Bros. Circus. *Harold Gorsuch Photo.*

The blacksmith shop on Barnum & Bailey's 1896 show seemed to be a gathering place. Note the handoperated blower next to the forge. *John Van Matre Collection.*

The Ringling Bros. Circus blacksmith shop around 1915. Harness maker is at work on the far left. There were blacksmiths in this crew, as well as horse-shoers. *Steve Albasing Photo.*

The Capewell Horse Nail Co. used to place advertisements in circus programs bragging that their product was used by the Big Show. *John Lentz Collection.*

In this 1929 photo the helper is about to drop the ring on double trees over the gooseneck on the wagon pole. The four-horse team will then spot the wagon in its proper place on the lot. *Dick & Peg Hemphill Collection.*

CHAPTER 7

Soft Lots

The *New York Clipper* and *Billboard Magazine* of the show world would report regularly on the various circuses as they toured the United States.

"Lot Bad—but business held up"

"Mud and Rain, turnaway crowds"

"Rained all day—big business"

"Lot a sea of mud—capacity house"

So read the lead lines—not a word about the draft horses and drivers that struggled to get the wagons onto the lot. Of course, rain, mud, wind, or sand made life miserable for everyone on the show—bar none. In 1929 when *Christy Bros. Circus* was in Great Falls, Montana, the show was buffeted by a severe storm. When the matinee was about two-thirds over, G.W. Christy, show owner, stopped the performance, dropped the front side-wall, and hustled the audience out. Five minutes later a terrific storm of wind, hail, and rain struck the tents and they all went down. Evening show was cancelled. The circus was loaded and moved to Shelby, but here it was still raining and the lot was a sea of mud. "All in a days work," was the attitude.

Ulrichsville, Ohio, 1910, *Ringling Bros.*: "lot so muddy that the show was delayed in getting loaded. As a consequence, show

arrived very late in Wheeling, West Virginia. The street parade was not given until the afternoon."

Quincy, Massachusetts, 1928, *Gentry Bros. Circus*: "had a bog lot which was more suitable for a water carnival than a circus."

Cheyenne, Wyoming, 1930, *Christy Bros.*: "a bad snowstorm which was rough on all animals."

Lorain, Ohio, 1928, *Hagenbeck-Wallace Circus*: had "the worst lot of the season. All the wagons had to be hookroped on to the lot."

Danville, Virginia, 1924, *Sells-Floto*: "moved onto a soft lot, put up all tents then cancelled the performance when a rainstorm turned the showgrounds into a marsh."

Reform, Alabama, 1925, *Christy Bros. Circus*: "we have had six days of continuous battling with rain, cold weather, muddy lots, and late arrivals, but never missed a performance. Here at Reform the lot was a swamp and the cookhouse wagon went in to the hubs. A bridge leading to the lot collapsed under the load of the pole wagon and things were at a standstill for a time. Another lot was secured adjoining the high school and two shows were eventually given."

Bedford, Indiana, 1927, *John Robinson Circus*: "the men got the cookhouse and menagerie tops up then called it quits as the lot was too soft. At 11:00 A.M. Manager Sam Dill called both shows off. It took until midnight to get the train loaded. Forty-two horses were required on some wagons. The stake driver sank to the tops of its wheels. Boss Hostler Jimmie Gould was up to the job."

Quitman, Georgia, 1926, *Christy Bros. Circus*: "we had a late arrival and no afternoon performance was given as the long road leading to the lot was loose sand a foot deep. The heavy wagons were moved in with great difficulty."

Wichita Falls, Texas, 1926, *Hagenbeck-Wallace Circus*: "a deluge of rain turned the roiling red dust into red mud. The big top shed water beautifully but outside was a sea of slush and mud."

Galveston, Texas, 1926, *Christy Bros. Circus*: "arrived late Sunday morning in the pouring rain (no shows scheduled for Sunday). It took until late at night to get the show onto the lot which was a veritable lake. Showday, Monday, and still raining. Downtown Galveston was flooded. At noon the sun came out and the parade was sent out. The wagons were plowing and the horses were splashing through hub deep water while the steam calliope player pecked out 'Sailing'."

Arkadelphia, Arkansas, 1925, *Hagenbeck-Wallace Circus*: "lot worst underfoot ever experienced. Thirty-six horses to a wagon."

Soft lots brought out the best in the Percherons and drivers. Soft lots of sand, sticky red clay, black gumbo, or spongy ground tested horses and men and wagons. Soft lots showed up the spunk and sticking power of the Percherons, the ingenuity of the Boss Hostler and his assistants, and the capability of the drivers. Soft lots demonstrated quickly the caring attitude these circus men had for their horses. Soft lots were hard on horses, men, and wagons. Fortunately, in the course of any season on any circus bad lot conditions were the exception.

The advance man who contracted for the lot always kept in mind what the condition of the lot would be in rainy weather. Sometimes he would bypass one spot in favor of another. Sometimes he had no choice but to contract for a less desirable showgrounds and hope for good weather.

Generally, all circuses played one-day stands and had to move on a daily basis to keep up with their billing. So, when adverse conditions were faced, horses and men were put to a hard test. And the show did move.

Here is an example of what could happen as told by Jack McCracken, an eight-horse driver for *Ringling Bros. and Barnum & Bailey* in 1924:

> The show was in New Castle, Pennsylvania, Saturday, June 28th. An afternoon performance was given when the drizzle turned into a hard rain. The ground began to show signs of softness and by the time the cookhouse wagons were taken off the lot late in the afternoon it was soft and muddy. As the rain increased in intensity, John Ringling called off the evening show and issued the order to take it down. Remember, this was about 6:00 P.M. Saturday afternoon, and we were scheduled to show in Pittsburgh the next day 45 miles to the south. We did not get the show off the New Castle lot and loaded on to the train until 6:30 P.M. Sunday. So we blew the two shows in Pittsburgh. We had mud like any of us had never seen before. It was raining, thundering, and lightning all night long. Horses and men worked through the night, stopping only briefly now and then to give the horses a rest and a bit of hay to nibble on.
>
> Number 31 Stringer wagon gave us the most trouble. It was a heavy one. At one point we had 64 Percherons on it set up this way. Pony Wilson had his eight on the wagon pole. Spot Griffin had his eight on the wagon pole gooseneck. I had my eight on the right front bull ring. Hans Fat had his eight on the second bull ring on the right side and Henry Brown had his eight on the third bull ring. Over on the left side of the wagon were three more eights—Curly Springer's, Dick Sells', and Big Top Dutch's. It was so bad that Wilson's wheelers were unhooked as the mud was just plowing up over their rumps. These 64 horses actually scull dragged the wagon off the lot. It was the worst night and day I ever spent in all my years with circuses.

The circus Pinky Barnes drove for in 1917 played Bloomington, Illinois. He said, "We had 72 horses on the pole wagon before we could slide and move the wagon onto solid ground."

Henry "Apples" Welsh recalled, "If we had a bad lot and one of the teams bogged down orders were not to fight it, as all we would do is tear up a lot of harness and gear. We simply waited until the Boss Hostler, or one of his assistants, saw our predicament. He would ride over, size up the extent of the problem, then whistle in one or more hook rope teams to get the wagon moving."

Harold Ingram was trainmaster on the *Sells-Floto Circus* in 1919. He commented as follows on a nightmare of a situation in Opelousas, Louisiana:

> The Show played Baton Rouge November 8 and we moved to Opelousas overnight. The sun was shining and we put on a beautiful street parade. It started to rain during the matinee and it kept up all during the evening performance. As soon as the show was over, all hands moved fast to get the tents down and everything packed into wagons. We got only four wagons off the showgrounds that night. We soon realized we were on a lot with no bottom.
>
> Our train stayed on the main line until midnight with the runs in place, but then the railroad had to switch the cars to a siding to let other trains through.
>
> Our men and horses struggled valiantly, yet the next day, November 10, we had only half the wagons off the lot. The management had the cookhouse set up in the railroad yards so the men could eat.
>
> Finally on the third day, November 11, we got the show loaded. We blew Pine Bluff and Little Rock and decided to close the season. We made three feed and water stops enroute to our Denver winter quarters. The draft stock gradually got back in shape. The rest while enroute did them a lot of good.

Joseph Brislin, a circus fan, reported a muddy lot scene in *White Tops* magazine. He witnessed the event June 22, 1937, when *Ringling Bros. and Barnum & Bailey Circus* played Lewiston, Maine. What makes his story interesting is the fact that he is viewing the episode from the outside looking in—not from the eyes of a circus man. Here are excerpts of his account:

> The lot was a bad one in wet weather, and the weather was wet. It had rained every day for three weeks. The showgrounds was large and grassy, surely ideal when the sun was shining, but with no bottom when soaked.
>
> The unloading crossing was a long haul from the lot. The train arrived at 6:45 A.M., many hours late. The cookhouse wagons arrived at the lot first. One of the wagons moved off the street and got about twenty-five feet onto the lot where it sank to its hubs. A second wagon tried and it met the same fate. All action ceased because it was necessary to assemble hook rope teams. Some sixty horses were thrown into the fray. This, of course, threw the unloading schedule into chaos because a team couldn't be in two places at once, and since they were needed on the lot there were few teams to haul the wagons from the runs. A bit later in the morning a local contractor was hired and supplied three trucks to help get the wagons to the lot—but it took horse power to spot each and every wagon. At last the cookhouse equipment was in place, and the tent began to rise into the rain and mist.
>
> Wagons began to pile up on the highway as there were not enough horses to haul them onto the lot in the usual orderly manner. The rain continued. The men were still wet from the night before. There was little conversation. It was close to 9:00 A.M. now. The menagerie top was slowly rising in the air. Cage wagons were pulled from the mud, hauled into line in the tent, then sank back into the mud to their hubs. The lot was now getting churned up, and the teams hauled wagons through ruts and earth stripped of all grass covering. It was pure, unadulterated mud.
>
> The heavy plank and chair wagons slithered onto the lot. It was interesting to see the hook rope teams at work. Like everything on a circus, things are named for the function they perform; thus a hook rope is just that, a rope, or chain, with a hook on the end that can be attached to steel rings on the corners of wagons.
>
> When a wagon came onto the lot it might sink evenly with all four wheels down to the hubs. It might sink on just one side, tilting the wagon at a crazy angle or, perhaps only one wheel would go down. No two wagons offered the same problem.
>
> Steve Finn was baggage stock boss assisted by Jim Doyle, Charlie Haley, and Phil Gardner—each boss taking charge of getting a wagon to its spot on the lot. Let us say that a wagon came onto the lot and sank and assume, too, that it was Charlie Haley's wagon. Charley would ride around the wagon to determine just how badly mired it was, the wagon load and size and footing for the team. After determining conditions, Charlie would hold up, let us say, eight fingers. This meant he wanted eight hook rope teams for this wagon. Perhaps he would decide that two elephants were needed and up would go two fingers to an elephant boss.
>
> The hook rope teams were used on the front of the wagon as a rule. It was explained to me that by using the front rings the front wheels would have a tendency to lift out of the mud. As soon as hauling power was supplied by as many as sixty horses, the front wheels eased up while two elephants pushed. They kept the wagon moving. Not once did I hear anything but firmest of commands, or orders, given in soft tones by any of the bosses. It was

"Nice going Slim," or, "That's just right, Highpockets." On this day the matinee was cancelled, but the evening show given. Loads of shavings had been dumped on the midway and in the tents.

By the time the performance was over it had stopped raining, but the mud was still there. The same kind of struggle to get off the lot was faced as to get on. Hook rope teams were required for every wagon. By 2:00 A.M. the big top was down, but it was 6:00 A.M. before the last wagon was on the flatcars. The ninety railroad car circus went 104 miles to Bangor and gave a matinee performance that day. The drivers and hostlers seemed to be greatly concerned about their horses through all this.

In this 1937 season the *Ringling Circus* travelled 15,427 miles and gave 404 performances in 31 states.

An unusually great photograph of forty horses moving a heavy wagon over soft ground. In this picture taken at Burlington, Vermont, July 9, 1916, on the Barnum & Bailey Circus, there are eight horses on the wagon and four hook-rope teams of 8-ups. The wagon is loaded with reserved seat stringers. *Ringling Museum of the Circus.*

The power of a horse when pulling a load is developed mainly in the hindquarters. Soft lots brought out all the good in drivers and horses. Here a heavy stringer wagon is in obviousdifficulty. The eight blacks on the wagon pole are getting some help from another long-string team. The driver of this team can be seen just ahead of the wheelers. The show and date of this photo are unknown, but the show is probably Ringling in the 1920s. *John Zweifel Collection*.

The enormous weight of the load of center poles dropped the rear wheel into a soft spot. This photo was taken in Texas in the 1920s on Ringling Bros. and Barnum & Bailey Circus. Note the lead bars and body poles hanging on the side of the wagon. *George Vilas Collection.*

When #84 Wagon on the Sells-Floto Circus sank into the mud, there was no big hassle. The driver looked down at the conditions, the team took advantage of the rest; orders were not to fight the situation and tear up harness and equipment. Soon the Boss Hostler would be over to look over the wagon, then whistle in as many chain teams as he thinks will be needed. *Author's Collection.*

The lot in Altus, Oklahoma, in 1926 was anything but the best. Gumbo like this complicates the spotting of the heavy wagons. *Robert Good Photo.*

Some lots were treacherous in that they looked solid, but the massive wagons seemed to find the soft spots. A situation like this is good evidence of why circus wagons were always "overengineered"—always built to withstand the worst possible conditions. This light plant wagon was pulled out with Percheron power. The electric light plant would be humming away soon, having been spotted in its proper place on the showgrounds. *M.D. McCarter Collection.*

The surefooted Percherons move a big wagon over the sloppy, slippery, muddy lot. All eight horses are pulling their share of the load. *John Zweifel Collection.*

When the driver of the water wagon felt his load sink, there he stopped. Logically, the elephants were brought to the wagon, where they were watered. This transferring of the load from tank to belly simplified the problem. When the water tank was empty, it became an easy task for the hook rope teams to move the wagon to solid ground. *John Zweifel Collection.*

Twenty horses move the wagon up the incline. The eight blacks are hooked to the gooseneck in front of the grey wheelers. RBB&B in South Bend, Indiana, in 1925. *Frank Updegrove.*

Note that the chain on the corner bull ring is taut, meaning that a hook rope team is assisting the 6-up or 8-up on this bogged down wagon. *Author's Collection.*

When the Yankee Robinson Circus pulled onto the showgrounds at Sidney, Montana, in 1912, trouble soon was in evidence. The soft lot added to the work for men and horses. *M.D. McCarter Collection.*

This is not a muddy lot, but it is soft. In this photo there are thirty-six horses—the six greys, eight on the wagon pole, eight blacks hook roping, then six more, then eight. The Boss Hostler is on the left of the wagon. *Anthony Kryzan Photo.*

A great action photo of hook roping. Three extra long-string teams are helping the blacks on the wagon. 1920s, RBB&B Circus. *George Vilas Collection.*

A good view of two hook rope teams (sometimes referred to as "chain teams") as they gather momentum. Cole Bros. Circus, Erie, Pennsylvania, 1940. *Jerry Booker Photo.*

In this 1912 photo of the Yankee Robinson Circus in Montana, the extreme flexibility of the wagon construction is demonstrated. The front running gear is turned completely under the wagon body. The pole points toward the right rear of the wagon. The horsepower on the gooseneck will pull the front end up and out of the mud hole. The right rear wheel will pivot in one spot, and the wagon will be brought to more solid ground. *W.D. McCarter Collection.*

Coordination is required so that all horses pull evenly. The drivers handled the Percherons with a steady hand. Cole Bros. Circus, Erie, Pennsylvania, 1939. *Jerry Booker Photo.*

The drivers always riding the near-wheelers are moving their teams across the lot. This is an excellent view of hook roping. Cole Bros., 1940 in Erie, Pennsylvania. *Jerry Booker Photo.*

Joe Wallace on the pinto was Boss Hostler on Cole Bros. Circus. This photo of him at work was taken in Erie, Pennsylvania, in 1939. *Jerry Booker Photo.*

Ringling's lot in Brooklyn in 1936 was far from level, creating some grades that required extra horse power to move wagons. *Circus World Museum, Baraboo, Wisconsin.*

At Chicago's lakefront showgrounds, four hook rope teams help the pole team move the wagon out of the mud and up the grade. All thirty-six horses are pulling steadily on the load—no seesawing and lunging. RBB&B in the 1930s. *Circus World Museum, Baraboo, Wisconsin.*

Ringling Bros. Circus in 1917 hit this soupy lot at Niagara Falls, New York. The next showtown was Buffalo, and there was never any doubt that the circus would be there. Any circus had to keep up with its billing. Conditions like those in the photo were taken in stride. The wagons were eventually spotted, the tent raised, and the performances given. Then everything taken down, and loaded into wagons, and the horses hauled them to the trains. *Steve Albasing Photo.*

Man and beast work together to get this Mighty Haag Show's wagon out of the mud. This photo was taken in 1912. *M.W. Organ Collection.*

The six horses on the big plank wagon are getting help from two eight-horse hook rope teams on this severe upgrade. The driver on the right is bringing his team around to be more in line with the direction in which the wagon is moving. RBB&B Circus at Wausau, Wisconsin, 1925. *Frank Updegrove Photo.*

As can be seen by the deep ruts in the ground, it is going to take horse power to move this pole wagon into position. Note that the wagon pole has been turned toward the cameraman. This cuts the heft of the load that the horses must move. Once the load is moving, the nimble footed horses can pick up speed and keep it coming. RBB&B Circus, 1920s. *George Vilas Collection.*

On occasion, elephants were put to work pushing wagons. *Steve Albasing Photo.*

There is lots of action in this photo of the Hagenbeck-Wallace Circus. However, the leaders on the wagon team are lagging, meaning that the wagon is rolling easily. *Author's Collection.*

When the Sparks Circus hit the showgrounds at Brockville, Ontario, in 1928, it took seven and one-half hours to get the show on the lot. The reason is quite evident in this photo. An eight-horse team on the wagon is assisted by three chain teams of 6-ups—twenty-six Percherons in all. *Eddie Jackson Photo*.

A truly great photo of horse power at work on a soft lot. Sparks Circus in 1928, Brockville, Ontario. *Eddie Jackson Photo.*

An interesting view from the wagon seat showing a hook rope team in place. *John Zweifel Collection.*

Sand can create an enormous drag on wagon wheels. Here on the Al G. Barnes Circus, a 6-up chain team is helping the eight on the wagon. *Jim McRoberts Collection*.

Through the roily loose sand, two eight-horse chain teams dig in to help the eight drafters on the big wagon. This photo was taken in 1924 on RBB&B Circus. *Frank Updegrove Photo*.

When the big wheels sink into the loose sand, the load that the team is pulling is multiplied. *Author's Photo.*

The bull ring shown will soon be put to good use when a chain team hooks on to roll this wagon out of the sand. The wheel is 6″ wide. *Author's Photo.*

A flash flood caused this grief for the Great Wallace Circus in Bucyrus, Ohio, in 1903. *Jim McRoberts Collection.*

Rains had softened this Hollywood, California, showgrounds, as the circus management soon realized when the big wagons rolled onto the lot on April 8, 1935. It was situations like this that tested the mettle of the draft stock and drivers. *Circus World Museum, Baraboo, Wisconsin.*

The horses were stabled each afternoon in tents. Here they were groomed, fed, watered and checked over. Generally, on the Circus, the stable tents were in a different town each day. *Author's Collection.*

CHAPTER 8

The Horse Tops

"I would never let my men make their horses get up to be curried and brushed if they happen to be lying down when it was their turn," commented Jake Posey, Boss Hostler on *Sparks Circus.*

When the daily task of setting up the circus was done, the Percherons were stabled in tents called "horse tops." These canvas stables were a place where the baggage stock could rest and be cleaned and fed. Now was the time of day that the harness was checked and cleaned. The drivers looked over the feet of their horses for a loose shoe, or even a missing shoe. They checked the horses over carefully for any blemish or cut that needed attention.

The drivers and helpers not only brushed and curried their animals, but washed them too. "We used lots of *Ivory* soap on the horses. The tails were regularly washed free of sand, grit, or mud. All the men had a deep sense of caring for their horses," remembered driver Frank Updegrove.

The tents used for stabling the horses varied in size from year to year and show to show. Here are a few sizes as examples:

John Robinson Circus in 1929:
2 Tents   34 x 98 feet

Sells-Floto Circus in 1929:
2 Tents   48 x 96 feet

Hagenbeck-Wallace Circus in 1925:
2 Tents   34 x 70 feet

Ringling Bros. and Barnum & Bailey Circus in the 1930s:
2 Tents   70 x 190 feet

Over the years, many variations appeared in stabling the horses, as each Boss Hostler had his pet methods. All were efficient and effective. Generally, picket lines were the favored method of tying the horses in place.

"Our draft stock was watered before and after each meal while in the stable," said Jake Posey. "We also watered the horses before they made their last trip to the train. When I was on the *Barnum & Bailey Show,* the rations for each Percheron per day was eighteen quarts of oats, twenty-five pounds of hay, and fifteen pounds of straw for bedding in the horse tent."

"When I drove for *Ringlings* in the early 1920s," said Frank Updegrove, "each of us drivers were given a cake of *Ivory* soap, brass polish, sponge, and bucket. We had to keep the horses clean, including their tails which we rolled up and dipped in a bucket of suds to remove all the dust, sand, grit, and manure. Every horse was curried and brushed on a daily basis. Occasionally a horse got a sore neck from, perhaps, a small cinder that got under the collar. When this occurred, the horse was immediately fitted with a breast strap arrangement until the neck was completely healed. Our show, under Boss Hostler Tom Lynch, was so particular about collars that one man was assigned to this important task. He was an expert and constantly checked the collars on hundreds of baggage horses. A horse fitted with a collar that is too big will cause rubbing sores, too small will choke off the horse's wind when he is pulling. My boss, Tom Lynch, loved his horses and insisted his drivers take the greatest care of them. A driver who was slipshod with the curry comb, or lazy with the brush, was very soon sent down the road. Another chore was cleaning harness. We had to wash the sweat and grime off the bridles, collars, back pads, and other leather parts. On circus baggage stock the halters were not removed when they were harnessed up. It was felt that this was the most efficient way to always have the halter in the right place when it was needed. When the big horses reached the stables and had their bridles and harness removed, the halters were always at hand complete with rope.

"Every afternoon each horse received half a bucket of oats. The drivers knew about when the call would come, and he would have his feed ready for his team. Then the Boss Hostler would holler out 'feed up,' and every horse would get his oats at the same time.

"Of course," Frank pointed out, "there was always a supply of good timothy hay in front of each horse while in the stable tent, and plenty of fresh water. When the horses were stabled and cleaned they got a bucket of fresh water. Again after graining them they were given a bucket of water. In the morning when the horses were working they got a good drink between trips from a canvas water trough that was set up on the street and filled with fresh cool water."

Frank Updegrove further observed, "When we removed the harness we always checked it over carefully. If a strap or buckle needed to be replaced we took it to the harness makers wagon to get it fixed right away."

The horse tops came down in late afternoon, usually. All canvas, center poles, quarter poles, side poles, picket lines, water buckets, pitch forks, wheelbarrows, and trunks with curry combs, brushes, medicine and other equipment and necessities were packed on and in wagons. The horses were then tied to the side of various wagons. Most often by 6:00 P.M. the wagons carrying the horse tops and cookhouse were on their way to the trains to be loaded as none of this equipment was needed for the evening show.

In Huntsville, Alabama, on Saturday, October 28, 1916, it was a beautiful fall day with a breeze blowing. *Ringling Bros. Circus* was in town and the big show was set up on North Washington Street, near the Southern Railway depot. The street parade had been given to enormous crowds that had swarmed into town to see the grand march and circus performance. By early afternoon thousands of townspeople had engulfed the showgrounds to see the matinee performance—15,000 it was estimated.

Nine-year-old Howard Harbin of nearby Maysville had come into town by horse and wagon with his family to see his first circus. Fifty-nine years later, in 1975, on the occasion of the *Ringling Circus'* first visit to Huntsville since 1916, Mr. Harbin was interviewed by the *Weekly Mercury* newspaper about that first visit. "As we approached the Big Top," Mr. Harbin said, "My mother suddenly grabbed me and herded us children close to the big tent. I can remember all this commotion. I could see smoke coming up from a little rise, a hill, just beyond the big top. Then we saw all these big horses coming at us at a full gallop from over the hill. We found out that just over the rise more than 100 draft horses were stabled in a tent. Two rows of horses had been tied to a picket line along the length of the tent with hay all along in front of the horses. Someone in the crowd had dropped a cigarette into the hay, and the breeze started the conflagration that raced down in front of the horses. I remember that there were 27 big horses charging over the rise at us with their hides ablaze and senses gone. Some of them had their eyes burned out; others with skin and meat hanging off of them, squealing as they ran scattered in all directions. When they were caught and stopped a man on horseback began shooting those so badly burned around the head. Mercifully, the horses dropped dead," concluded Mr. Harbin.

The *Birmingham [Alabama] News* carried this account at the time of the fire of the sickening tragedy to the baggage stock. The headline stated "47 Horses Die when Circus Tent is Swept by Fire." The story continued, "The fire struck the stable tent just before the opening of the afternoon performance. More than 50 horses were badly burned before they could be cut loose, and of this number, 30 were dead when the first count of the casualties was made. Others were terribly burned about the head; many were permanently blinded and a dozen were shot and put out of their misery. Every veterinarian in the city was busy Saturday night and Sunday. At least 15 more animals will probably have to be killed. It was estimated that each of the *Ringling* draft animals was worth $350.00, and with 47 dead, the loss is close to $16,450.00. This does not include the loss of the tent and harness estimated at $70.00 for each horse. No performing horses were lost, and the performance went on one-half hour after the tragedy, as if nothing had occurred.

"Ninety new horses were engaged by telegraph to be delivered at the Mississippi town (Clarksdale) where the show is booked to appear Monday, Oct. 30th."

That statement "ninety new horses were engaged by telegraph" is most interesting. It was as if Percherons trained for circus work were as easy to come by as picking apples off a tree. It turned out, in this case, they were. In one of his many letters, Jake Posey, who was Boss Hostler of the *Hagenbeck-Wallace Circus* at that time, reminisced, "Our circus closed its season October 26. All the baggage stock had been turned out to pasture near the winter quarters in West Baden, Indiana. On October 28, Ed Ballard, circus owner, called me and said to catch up 100 head, fit them with harness, and load them into stock cars. It turned out that on this date the *Ringling Bros. Circus* playing Huntsville, Alabama, had a fire in a horse tent. Forty head were burned to death and forty more had to be destroyed. The big problem my men and I had was to go out into strange fields and catch up the horses in the dark. Ballard said, 'Don't wait for daylight.' I was then ordered to send my 100 head with Eddie Evans, Assistant Boss Hostler, to the Ringling's for the rest of the season."

It is interesting how quickly a tragedy could wash out the ill feeling created by billing wars and territorial fights of past years between these two shows. As luck would have it, West Baden was only about 375 miles to the north.

A sequel to this calamity turned up in the *Huntsville Weekly Mercury* on November 1. The article stated, "City and County came to the rescue of a local man who had the big job of burying circus horses. The burned carcasses of the dead horses killed from the effects of the stable tent fire Saturday, while *Ringling Brothers Circus* was here, were being removed yesterday by every conveyance possible to procure.

"There were nearly a hundred to remove, and as the day was warm it was anticipated that trouble would result if the carcasses were not speedily removed.

"The bodies were hauled to city-owned grounds and a crew of men was busy burying them. The circus left men here to look after the burying of the horses. They had made arrangements with a local man to do the job for $100.00. He was attempting to carry out his contract, but it was plainly evident that he had undertaken a job he could not finish. Rather than allow the matter to grow into a problem, Judge McDonnell and Mayor Terry went to the scene and put to work every available wagon and truck to get the work speedily through. Arrangements will be made to get the Circus management to pay for this work, and there is no doubt this will be done."

Baggage stock tent of 1899 on the Ringling Bros. Circus. It was in these tents (called "horse tops") that the draft horses spent the afternoons being groomed, washed, and checked over. They always had a supply of timothy hay in front of them. *Author's Collection.*

In 1897, when this photo was taken in the Ringling Bros. horse tops, a number of the Percherons were lying down. Note that the tent's side wall is up. This protected the horses from rain or cold winds. If it was a warm, balmy day, the side walls would be removed. *Author's Collection.*

Frank Updegrove, six-horse driver for the Ringling Circus, had this photo taken of himself and his horses. Many of the photos in this book were taken by him as he travelled the United States with the big circus. *Frank Updegrove Collection.*

While this photo was taken in Alma, Michigan, in 1925 on the Ringling Bros. and Barnum & Bailey Combined Shows, no matter which of scores of cities the circus played that year, the inside of the horse tents would look the same. Note the harness hanging from hooks on the sidepoles. The horses were tethered to a picket line. *Frank Updegrove Photo.*

A single day's supply of hay and grain for the horses. This photo was taken in Chicago in 1925 while the Ringling Circus was there. *Frank Updegrove Photo.*

On occasion, when the show trains arrived late, everything got behind schedule. In this instance, because the sun was shining and it was a warm day, the horse tops were never put up. The baggage stock was tied to picket lines, as seen here. The horses have just been fed their allotment of oats. *Frank Updegrove Photo.*

Draft horse tent on RBB&B Circus. Sacks of grain, bales of hay, pails, drivers at ease, harness neatly hung on sidepoles, some laundry drying in the sun—this scene would be repeated every afternoon but in a different city practically every day. *Jerry Booker Photo.*

Taking it easy in the draft horse tents. This is one of the tents used by Ringling Bros. and Barnum & Bailey in the 1930s. *Jerry Booker Photo.*

Catastrophe struck the Al G. Barnes Circus in 1926 when a powerful wind blew down the horse tent. The steadiness of the draft stock can be seen. Some have been taken out from under the canvas and stand quietly. Others still stand with the canvas draped over them, waiting to be rescued. *Mike Tschudy Collection.*

Due to the blowdown, it took a few days to repair the damaged tent. The circus continued to move, of course, to keep up with its billing. Meanwhile, the draft stock was picketed in the open, as seen here. Al G. Barnes Circus, 1926. *Mike Tschudy Collection.*

Cedar Rapids, Iowa, July 24, 1924, showing all the baggage stock of the Ringling Bros. and Barnum & Bailey Combined Shows. *Frank Updegrove Photo.*

Boss Hostler Red Finn stands at the left while three Percheron drafters pose for this publicity photo. *Circus World Museum, Baraboo, Wisconsin.*

Because of the a late arrival in town, the Kit Carson Wild West Show did not put up its horse tops. *Harry Armstrong.*

The receipt/invoice on the left reads:

Baggage 80.00
Ring Stock ... 25.00
Menagerie ... 26.00
Cars for Elephants 11.00
31 4200   Total,   - Hay @ 1.10 | 156 | 20

Lot ....
Baggage 30.00
Ring Stock ... 12.00
Menagerie ... 600
48.00   Total,   - Straw @ .75 | 36 | 00

Baggage 190
Ring Stock ... 35
Menagerie ...
222   Total,   - Oats @ 85 | 188 | 70

1300   Bran @ 2.00 | 26 | 00

1200 alfalfa meal | 30 | 00
1 Load Shaving | 7 | 00
J. E. Stroud $443 90

TOTAL, ...

Date Aug 1 - 18
RECEIVED payment in full of the above.   Paid
O.K. W. L. Carr   M Strout
$443.90   FEED CONTRACTOR. Aug 1-18

Each day the twenty-four-hour man of the circus arranged for the final purchase and delivery of hay and oats to the showgrounds. Here is the order that Ringling Bros. had given a feed dealer in Clinton, Iowa, on August 1, 1918. Note that the circus ordered, for the baggage stock, four tons of hay, one and one-half tons of straw, and 190 bushels of oats for this day. *Author's Collection.*

Cole Bros. Circus, fifty head of draft horses at Middletown, Ohio, 1940. *Harold Gorsuch Photo.*

Seen here is the draft stock of Barnum & Bailey Circus in 1915 tethered to picket lines. *Author's Collection.*

An 8-up being harnessed and about to leave the horse top late in the afternoon. Note that the lines for each team are still neatly coiled and tied to the hame of each off horse. Hagenbeck-Wallace Circus, 1930s. *Harold Gorsuch Photo.*

Headaches on the travelling circus come in many forms. Caught in a sudden hailstorm with its tents up, the draft horse department suffered severe damage. 1920s. *John Zweifel Collection.*

Once the horse tents are down, the teams are tied to various wagons, as in this 1937 photo. *Author's Photo.*

The draft stock would stand quietly. Sometimes they would be given a bite of hay to nibble on while they waited for their driver to show up. RBB&B, 1937, Milwaukee. *Author's Photo.*

In Dayton, Ohio, an old iron fence became a convenient place to tie the baggage stock in the late afternoon. RBB&B Circus, 1938. *Harold Gorsuch Photo.*

The Percherons would frequently lie down in harness while waiting for an assignment. 1940 photo. *Harold Gorsuch Photo.*

CHAPTER 9

In the Street Parade

When the circus paraded its plumed horses, exciting cages of exotic wild animals, enormous bandwagons, beautiful equestrians, stirring bands, magnificent tableaux, zebras, camels and ponderous elephants, and the raucous steam calliope down the main street, townspeople knew without a lingering doubt something the kids knew for sure for two weeks—"Today Was Circus Day."

The advertising crew of the big show had plastered barns, sheds, and fences with huge colorful posters that proclaimed when the circus would be in town. Additional posters were hung in store windows, and the newspapers carried large advertisements.

On circus day the street parade was used as a nail clincher. It was a form of advertising that played on the eye, the ear, and the nose. It really stirred up the population. Never in history was there a form of advertising that was so powerfully gripping. It verged on being irresistible, and the street parade had Percherons in teams of four or six. There were teams of eight on the big tableaux. Ten or twelve Percherons were on the major bandwagons. Occasionally, a big circus would use twenty-four Percherons on a wagon just for show. The biggest splash of all was forty Percherons on one wagon driven by one man.

Nineteen hundred twenty-one was the beginning of the end of the street parade era. In this season, *Ringling Bros. and Barnum & Bailey Circus* gave up the daily grand march. Showgrounds were too far away from the downtown. Auto and truck traffic was snarled by the horse-drawn pageant. Stop-and-go lights began to appear and chopped up the continuity of the event. Macadam pavements on hot July and August days got too soft for the massive steel-tired wagons. The end of the horse-drawn circus parade was close at hand.

Billboard Magazine reported the following story:

"What's become of the old Circus Parades?" Mr. Charles Ringling was asked by a Canton, Ohio, reporter when his show played there in 1923. "They have died out," Mr. Ringling replied. "At least as far as our show is concerned. There are two reasons: First, the show is too big to allow us time for a parade. Second, the automobile has virtually driven us off the big city streets. Imagine if you can what would happen if all traffic on the downtown streets was tied up for two hours—the time required for one of our parades to pass. You would have people missing trains and a general demoralization of traffic. The Circus Parade is a vanished institution."

Although Canton Mayor C.C. Curtis issued an edict recently that a circus must put out a parade before it will be given a license to show, he let the big circus in and out without any controversy over the issue. Canton expected a parade and there was much disappointment when the announcement was made the day previous that this feature would be eliminated.

Gradually, over the next twenty years, all of the major railroad circuses followed suit. The end came in 1939 when *Cole Bros. Circus* paraded that season for the last time.

The horse-drawn circus street parade was just another part of the day's work for the draft stock. These marches most often were scheduled at 11:00 A.M. By then, if everything went right, the circus would be on the showgrounds with tents in the air. Each long-string team was assigned to the same wagon each day. Large 12- to 18-inch feather plumes would be attached to bridles and sometimes hames of each horse.

For certain teams on the #1 Bandwagon, perhaps a hame housing decorated with brass letters and spots would be added. Occasionally, other decorative pieces of harness such as kidney drops were added. There were a few occasions when a circus would harness the number-one team in a special way. For example, white patent-leather harness on a black team, or red leather on a grey team.

In one of his many letters, long-string driver Henry "Apples" Welsh reflected on the various extra-special teams he remembered:

> In 1908 on the *101 Ranch Wild West Show* I had eight black mules pulling a big white and gold bandwagon for parade. But I think the prettiest band team I ever put together was for Al F. Wheeler on the *Wheeler Bros. Show* in 1916—eight coal blacks. I designed the harness for them; white patent leather and all nickle-plated trimmings. It was made by *Worth Bros.* in Baltimore. All the horses wore 18-inch white feather plumes on their bridles which really flashed them up.
>
> The nicest ten-horse team I ever put together was for Mr. Al Ringling in 1911 on the *4-Paw-Sells Show*. Mr. Al said they were as nice a matched team as he ever saw. Albert Crisp was the driver. I had 160 horses to pick from. The same team went to the Ringling Show in 1912.

One of the last horse-drawn street parades was given by *Hagenbeck-Wallace Circus* in 1934. It was quite an impressive march that included 154 head of draft horses, but it was not up to the whopping events that were given in the teen years by the big shows. Here is their 1934 parade order:

Two mounted, women flag bearers
Four mounted women, American flags
Bandwagon, ten horses
No. 31 den, lions, four horses
No. 71 Mother Goose tab., eight horses
No. 12 den, tigers, four horses
Polar bear den, six horses
Five mounted women
No. 8 den, deer, four horses
No. 37 band, six horses
No. 32 den, eight horses
Tandem, woman driving
No. 4 den, four horses
Six mounted women
No. 101 small chimes, eight ponies
No. 9 den, deer, four horses
Two four-horse chariots
Joe Lewis and mule
No. 46 den, six horses
Five mounted women
No. 14 den, hippo, eight horses
No. 6 den, hippo, eight horses
No. 38 Ceylon tab, six horses
Four mounted women
No. 5 den, four horses
No. 100, air calliope, four horses
Tab. No. 75, Red Riding Hood, six horses
Tandem, two horses, woman driver
No. 11 den, bears, four horses
No. 102 Clown band, six horses
Two tandem teams, four horses
No. 19 den, six horses
No. 16 den, six horses

Three mounted men
No. 41 tab., Mickey Mouse, band, six horses
No. 18 den, six horses
No. 3 den, four horses
No. 103 chimes, six horses
Wild West mounted, 21 people
No. 67 tab., Scotch band, four horses
Six ponies, led
Ten zebras, led
Four camels, led
No. 59 snake den, glass, eight camels
Thirty-one elephants
No. 44 Calliope, six horses

When a show came to town and paraded its wares down the main street, people had various "rule of thumb" measurements by which they decided on the size and scope of the circus. How many elephants? They were easy to count and were impressive. How many draft horses? Were there many two-horse teams, or were they mostly six- and eight-horse teams? These sleek Percherons were always a sight to behold. However, when a bandwagon was pulled by twenty-four horses, or forty horses, all driven by one man, then the townspeople knew it was a truly big show in town. The forty-horse hitch was probably the most spectacular parade feature of all time. The first show to pull this stunt was *Spalding & Rogers Circus* in 1848. *Nixon and Kemp Circus* copied the attraction in the 1850s and, in fact, in 1858 advertised that a woman would drive their Forty. Through the 1860s and 1870s a half-dozen or more shows paraded a forty-horse hitch. *Barnum & Bailey* was the last circus to display a team of this size, and that was during the seasons of 1903 and 1904.

Jake Posey, one of the drivers who drove the Forty for *Barnum & Bailey,* said in one of his many letters:

No, I did not use pebbles to throw at a lagging horse. I had two big hands full of leather and no room for anything else. I had two men on the wagon with me. One was to keep the lines straight. You see, when I was going around a corner I would take up about twenty feet of reins. When I was around the corner and the team straightened out, I had to let the slack run through my fingers. If there should be a twist in one of the reins it would knock them all out of my hand. The other man worked the wheel brake. It is really amusing to read some of the articles in magazines about the Forty. I was making parade in Aberdeen, Scotland, and we passed a large brewery. The workers out front saw my brakeman winding up the brake wheel. One of the workers said, "Look, he is winding up the reins." I read many articles just as ridiculous.

The end of the forty-horse team spectacular came about in this way. Henry "Apples" Welsh wrote, "About the Forty, I was with the *Barnum & Bailey Show* in 1904. In the spring of 1905 at our Bridgeport winter quarters, I was one of Tom Lynch's assistants and he and I drove the Forty the last time it was hitched up to exercise. He drove the lead-twenty and I drove the wheel-twenty. All were bay Percherons with black manes and tails. Then the word came from Mr. Bailey, 'No more parades.' We put the harness away, and it was never used again."

Barnum & Bailey did give up the parade but soon put it back on the street, but the Forty was reduced to a 24-horse team.

Long-string driver Will Brock wrote, "In 1909 when I was on the *Barnum & Bailey Show* we opened the season in Chicago in the Coliseum, then went to Champaign for our first stand under canvas. Here the 24-horse hitch of greys were put together for the first time as a team, and none of the horses ever had a band behind them before. Jim Thomas mounted to the seat, gathered up the lines, and made the parade as though the horses were veterans. This was old Jim Thomas, a real driver."

After a seemingly long wait, here she comes. The eight Percherons clip-clopping on the brick pavement and the brass band playing bring real excitement as the John Robinson Circus parades by the kids on the curb. Note the near leader—ears erect, looking at the balloon. *Jim McRoberts Collection.*

As the gold-leafed tableau rolls down the street, the boys run alongside, stimulated by the sights, sounds, and smells of the grand march. *Jim McRoberts Collection.*

The cage wagon, pulled by six drafters with bobbing red feather plumes, rumbles down the brick street. *Author's Collection.*

As can be seen here, this huge wagon is being powered only be the wheel team and the four-horse body pole team. The six and eight-horse body pole teams and the leaders are dragging their body poles and lead bars. On an uphill climb, all horses would be working, as will be the case when the wagon hits soft showgrounds. This driver has his team perfectly lined up. Ringling Bros., circa 1915. *Steve Albasing Photo.*

A lightweight team of bays is hitched to this Sells-Floto tableau about ready to leave the lot for the daily parade. *Hugo Zeiter Collection.*

The robes, or blankets as they were called, indicate music, and so the team is pulling a bandwagon. Note that the horses are wearing tri-colored feather plumes, probably red, white, and blue. *Gene Baxter Collection.*

Crowds jam the curbs to watch the parade pass. It created an exhilaration that was hard to surpass, culminating in going to the circus—and that was the exact purpose of this form of advertising. *Circus World Museum, Baraboo, Wisconsin.*

Ten dapple grey Percherons in perfect line walk along the brick street pulling a big bandwagon. *Circus World Museum, Baraboo, Wisconsin.*

This four-horse team, circa-1892, is of a lighter weight than was generally used twenty and thirty years later, when wagons were more massively constructed. The three-man crew for this Sells Bros. steam calliope are the driver, the player, and (on the right) the boilerman, or fireman. *Ringling Museum of the Circus.*

In 1907, when a Campbell Bros. Circus played Fairbury, Nebraska, the parade passed through a shaded residential area on the way to the business district. *J.W. Beggs Collection.*

The ornate cage is on the John Robinson Circus. The greys appear to be a team of drafters, while the chestnuts appear to be lightweight performing horses. Ordinarily, the heavier team should be the wheelers, but here they are needed to steady the 4-up. *Author's Collection.*

Ringling Bros. Circus parading in Norwood, Ohio, in 1916. The red feather plumes were 18″ long and were fitted onto bridles. Plumes were standard equipment on all draft horses when they paraded. *Circus World Museum, Baraboo, Wisconsin.*

The harness worn by the Percherons in parade was the same that they wore earlier in the morning when they were hauling wagons to the show-grounds and spotting them. This year, 1916, the Ringling Bros. Hostler did not roach the manes. This was his prerogative. The cage contained tigers. Note the white pith helmets and matched uniforms of men, so typical of this circus. *Circus World Museum, Baraboo, Wisconsin.*

The last season that the Cole Bros. Circus paraded was 1939. This was the end of this great advertising event as far as the big rail-road shows were concerned. Seen here are eight beautifully matched dapple greys pulling the United States bandwagon. *Circus World Museum, Baraboo, Wisconsin.*

Like threading a needle—these eight Percherons, pulling the heavy steam calliope in Ringling Bros. Circus Parade of 1907, show their even temperaments as they move through the crowds. Nothing seemed to bother them, even fluttering white dresses, weaving umbrellas, or a handkerchief pulled out to mop a brow. This lack of skitterishness was one of the many assets that circusmen found in the Percheron horse. *Ringling Museum of the Circus.*

The Ringling tiger den moves along easily, as does the string of cage wagons ahead. The photo shows the well-fed and well-groomed condition of the draft stock. 1916, Norwood, Ohio. *Circus World Museum, Baraboo, Wisconsin.*

In 1911 the Forepaugh-Sells Bros. Circus bandwagon, pulled by fine young team of Percherons, threads its way through the jammed streets. *Circus World Museum, Baraboo, Wisconsin.*

Not all baggage stock pulled wagons in parade. Some circuses used them for a mounted band. In parade, the musicians guided the horses around corners with reins fastened to the stirrups. This kept their hands free to play their instruments. The musicians also learned to turn their instruments sideways, as the clarinet players are doing. If the horse tossed his head up, it would not hit the instrument. This is Ringling Bros. Circus' mounted band of the 1905 era. *J.W. Beggs Collection.*

In 1900, the Harris Nickle Plate Shows had this mounted band in their street parade using baggage stock. *Author's Collection.*

In 1857, this advertisement appeared in the newspapers along the route of Nixon & Kemp's Circus for the forty-horse team driven by one man. *Author's Collection.*

The crowds packed the streets to see the Barnum & Bailey Circus parade in 1898. This photo, taken in Nottinghan, England, is an excellent view of the forty-horse hitch. The horses were matched bays with black manes and tails. *Author's Collection.*

The Barnum & Bailey Greatest Show on Earth

SECTION 1 - SHOWING THE GREAT 40 HORSE TEAM AND PONDEROUS TABLEAU BAND WAGON OF THE TWO HEMISPHERES. THIS ONE VEHICLE AND TEAM REPRESENTING AN OUTLAY OF OVER $50,000

THE WORLD'S LARGEST, GRANDEST, BEST, AMUSEMENT INSTITUTION

This circus paraded a forty-horse team of matched bays in the United States in 1903 and 1904. Here is a poster advertising the great event showing the twenty-eight-foot long Two Hemispheres Bandwagon. *Circus World Museum, Baraboo, Wisconsin.*

To dress up some teams for parade purposes, the circus would provide fancy hame housings, body drops, and kidney drops, as seen here on the Hagenbeck-Wallce Show. It appears that these horses are provided with a special brass button-trimmed bridle. This might have been the lead bandwagon in the parade. *Author's Collection.*

In 1917, Hagenbeck-Wallace used this white and gold bandwagon pulled by twelve black Percherons. Jack McCracken, long-string driver, wrote about this team. "We had to change bridles for the parade. Also had white back pads and housings over the hames. Sure was lots of trappings to change every day for parade. These special trappings were carried in the bandwagon, which was in charge of two men. Each piece had a separate flannel-lined sack to cover them. After each day's parade, they were cleaned and polished and put in these sacks. Eddie Moore (Tulsa Eddie) drove the team. It was an 8-up in baggage, and they added a 4-up for parade, making it a twelve-horse team. All were coal black with white trappings and white 18″ plumes on the hame housings. Really was a swell parade unit." *Jim McRoberts Collection.*

Ringling Bros. used twenty-four greys on their huge Swan Bandwagon in the "teen" years. Even in the days when the horse was so commonplace, these beautifully matched and well-trained horses were outstanding attractions. *Richard Conover Collection*.

This is the hame housing used by Christy Bros. in the 1920s. The shiny brass letters and buttons flashed up the work harness. *Author's Photo.*

The black Percherons on this Barnum & Bailey bandwagon are wearing a special white leather harness and bridles for their parade assignment. Fancy harness like this was the exception rather than the rule. *Ringling Museum of the Circus.*

The John Robinson's Peacock bandwagon in 1906 was pulled by some well-trapped draft horses. *Albert Conover Collection.*

The blind on the bridle on the big shows usually carried a brass letter signifying the circus "R" for Ringling, as shown, or perhaps "RB" for Ringling-Barnum. These bridles were worn by the Percherons while spotting wagons on the lot, or in the street parade. *Author's Photo.*

In its heyday in 1915, this hame housing decorated a harness on the Hagenbeck-Wallace Circus. The cast brass initials "H-W" added a touch of elegance to the harness for the street parade. *Author's Collection.*

In 1905, Pawnee Bill's Wild West Show used very elaborate and highly decorative harnesses for the team on their enormous bandwagon. *John Van Matre Collection.*

The Percherons with 18″ long red feather plumes in their bridles pulling their load of the steam calliope bring up the rear, as was traditional, of the Ringling Bros. Circus street parade of 1909. *Ringling Museum of the Circus.*

These brass ornaments are from the work harness of the Ringling Bros. and Barnum & Bailey baggage stock of the 1930s. The various decorative pieces were standard catalog items. The circus used just enough brass to flash up an otherwise drab leather harness. *Author's Collection.*

When the Carl Hagenbeck Wild Animal Show hit the road in 1905, some of their teams in parade carried special hame housings with cast brass lettering, as shown here. *Author's Collection.*

A team of Percheron draft horses, ears erect, carry the showgirls, who are riding sidesaddle. This is the street parade of the 1911 Forepaugh-Sells Bros. Circus in Monroe, Wisconsin. These greys were versatile and looked good in this capacity. They also hauled big wagons. *Circus World Museum, Baraboo, Wisconsin.*

There are sixteen Percherons in this photo. Ten are pulling wagons, and six are carrying pretty showgirls in stunning wardrobe. Most likely, earlier in the morning these Percherons were a 6-up hauling a wagon to the showgrounds. The date sheet on the corner building proclaims Gollmar Bros. Circus coming to town, Monday July 31st (1922). *Author's Collection.*

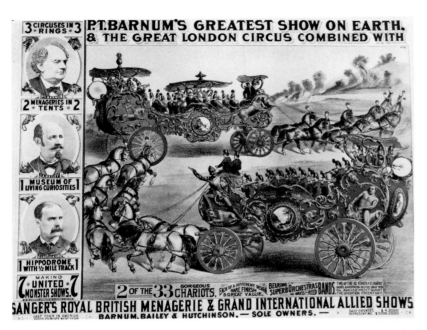

The draft horses edged into the advertising when the circus ordered posters of parade features. The artist had to include horses if vehicles were illustrated, although in their efforts to make the big wagons look enormous, the mighty Percherons almost looked diminutive. 1882. *Cincinnati Art Museum.*

John O'Brien's 1872 Show moved overland from town to town. To illustrate the street parade, the artist had to include the draft horses; however, they appear to be a bit on the snappy side after a night of plodding over the dirt roads. *New York Historical Society.*

The draft stock had some work to do around winterquarters—perhaps haul manure out or haul hay in. Some horses were put out to winter pasture. *Gene Baxter Collection.*

CHAPTER 10

At Winter Quarters

And now the season is over and the big railroad circuses head back to their respective winter quarters. Macon, Georgia; Bridgeport, Connecticut; Denver, Colorado; Baraboo, Wisconsin; Peru, Indiana; Beaumont, Texas; Baldwin Park, California, and many other towns over the years have been home base for circuses.

Frank Updegrove, a long-string driver of the 1920s, reflected that "when the circus got back to winter quarters, the Boss Hostler would select a few teams to keep at quarters for various daily chores. The rest of the stock was put out to pasture for the winter after their shoes were removed."

In the fall of 1928 *Ringling Bros. and Barnum & Bailey Combined Shows* began using their new winter quarters in Sarasota, Florida. The move created many advantages, not the least of which was sunshine and warm weather. There were problems in this move; namely, Florida hay had little nutritional value. Four hundred or more horses ate a lot of hay every day. So the hay was shipped in from the north. The next year John Ringling made a move that startled the show world. He purchased the *American Circus Corporation*, which was comprised of five major railroad circuses. The winter quarters for the Corporation shows was Peru, Indiana, where good timothy hay was no problem.

Early-on, John Ringling started the policy of shipping his baggage stock to Indiana for the winter, where there was ample supply of hay and oats. In addition, the colder temperatures were better for the drafters than the hot, humid Florida weather.

In October of 1932 *Billboard Magazine* ran a brief notice datelined Peru, Indiana: "Steve Finn, Assistant Boss Hostler on the *Ringling Show* with 60 drivers and 300 horses arrived from Sarasota on a special train of 15 stockcars and one coach *Michigan*. With the placing of the baggage stock on the circus farm, all drivers but four were released for the winter."

In these years it must have been an exhilarating sight to see perhaps 700 to 800 grade-Percherons stabled, or on pasture, at the Peru winter quarters farm.

Billboard in November 1934 ran this item, "Breaking a custom of past years, the *Ringling* baggage stock will be kept in the Sarasota winter quarters this winter."

The chores at winter quarters for some of the Percheron teams were many and varied. There might be railroad cars to be moved in and out of repair shops. Wagons had to be moved into the paint shop, then out again. There was always something to haul —a team might take a wagon to the freight depot; another to pick up meat for the wild animals. After all, it was at winter quarters where a circus grew, changed, refurbished, and rebuilt. So there was plenty of action for the draft horses.

As spring approached, the teams that were out on pasture were brought in, matched up, harnessed, and exercised after they were shod. The horses had to be hardened up to be ready to hit the road.

Billboard Magazine would frequently run short comments about this type of activity. In the April 13, 1935, issue it read: "Approximately 150 head of baggage horses are now stabled at winter quarters of *Cole Bros. Circus* in Rochester, Indiana. Blackie Diller has his crew of 8, 6, and 4-horse drivers working out with their teams daily."

January 4, 1930: "Assistant Boss Hostler, Charlie Rooney at Peru winter quarters received a shipment of 50 head of first-rate draft horses. A number of long-string drivers are on hand."

December 1, 1928: "Tom Lynch, half century in the circus business, is as usual in charge of the Draft Horse Dept. with a full crew under him at the new *Ringling-Barnum* winter quarters in Sarasota, Florida. This was the big show's first winter in Florida, having wintered in the past in Bridgeport, Connecticut."

February 23, 1929, Granger, Iowa: "Joe Lloyd, Supt. of baggage stock for *Robbins Bros. Circus* spent several days at the farm overseeing the return of the big horses from pasture and organizing the work of conditioning them for the summer season."

February 6, 1926, Beaumont, Texas: "*Christy Bros. Circus*: For the first time in 30 years there was snow here last Saturday. More than six inches fell and it raised havoc with the show horses that were turned out to pasture. They suffered from the blizzard and two died before they were brought into winter quarters and stabled in a barn."

September 24, 1932, Baldwin Park, California: "*Al G. Barnes Circus*: All baggage stock, in charge of Jake Posey, has been turned out on a beautiful 1,000 acre pasture in the foothills about ten miles from winter quarters."

February 12, 1927, Macon, Georgia: "*Sparks Circus*: Jake Posey has his big stock quartered in a new 70-foot x 270-foot brick building. He is assisted by Steve Brown and a crew of old-time long-string drivers."

February 4, 1928, Granger, Iowa: "*Robbins Bros. Circus*: A carload of first-rate drafters from *Barrett & Zimmerman* in St. Paul was unloaded this week and housed in the baggage stock stables."

Jim "Mushmouth" Traver had been a long-string driver for ten years with *Ringling Bros.* When he showed up for work in early April in 1910, he was given a team of eight young and green horses to break. Let Traver tell the story:

> With my helper we harnessed the horses and hitched them to an empty plank wagon. Even empty, this long wagon had plenty of heft to it. Well, we drove down Water Street (in Baraboo, Wisconsin) and out of town. The horses seemed to steady down as we went along until a damn fool farm dog started yapping alongside them. These horses just took off. My helper had tightened the brakes, but these young horses just sort of took the bit in their teeth and ran. I eased them off the dirt road we were on and into a field. Being spring, the ground was kind of soft and the plank wagon with its 5-inch-wide wheels sort of sank into the soil. I just wheeled these spunky horses into a big circle and let them run. When they pooped out and wanted to stop I kept them going a while longer. That team, when they finally stopped, were blowing and heaving and sweated up. We got off the wagon and walked along the horses talking to them. When they cooled off a bit and had stopped blowing, we drove back onto the road, into town and to winter quarters at a nice slow steady walk. I drove that team all that season and never had a bit of trouble. This eight was a good-looking iron-grey bunch. They were excellent.

John M. Kelley, attorney for the *Ringling Bros.* and their circus interests, reflected back to the evening before the circus was to load up and leave Baraboo for Chicago, the opening stand for 1910. Kelley said:

> All the drivers were at the corner tavern on Water Street next to the winter quarters in Baraboo, Wisconsin. They were all having a good time and, as usual, drinking a bit too much. One of them, a gent named Silver Haired Irish, was being looked for by the police for some small infraction of the law. An unsuspecting cop walking the beat came into the saloon and saw Irish at the bar with his buddies. The cop made the mistake of trying to take Irish out of the saloon. The boys moved in. They removed his pistol from his holster, at which the cop became abusive. At this point a couple of the boys went to winter quarters and brought back a two-wheeled

shifting cage. Next they took off the policeman's coat and pants and put him into the cage. The uproarious gang wheeled the cart a half a block to the Baraboo River and pushed it in, tieing it to a tree on the bank. I can't tell you how long the unfortunate cop shivered in the cage, but I know that bright and early the next morning I was summoned by Mr. Al Ringling to get up to see the Chief of Police on the double and make peace. Mr. Al reminded me the show was loading out, and they needed every last long-string driver.

Barnum & Bailey Circus maintained winterquarters in Bridgeport, Connecticut, for many years. The baggage stock was stabled in a two-story building. The horses were on the ground floor, as shown. The second floor had a harness shop, storage room, and sleeping quarters for the men. *Author's Collection.*

Some of the Big Show's draft stock was pastured outside the city of Bridgeport. These horses were too well trained to circus work to sell in the fall with the idea of buying fresh horses in the spring. Then, too, good stock of the age, size, and color that the circusmen wanted was difficult to find. *John Zweifel Collection.*

Ringling Bros. and Barnum & Bailey Combined Shows wintered from 1919 through the spring of 1927 in Bridgeport, Connecticut. Here are some of the Percherons lazing in the sun. *John Zweifel Collection.*

This is the winterquarters of Ringling Bros. and Barnum & Bailey. When these two enormous shows combined for the 1919 season (and forever after), they used the Brideport quarters. Seen here are the draft horse switching a heavy coach. 1925. *Frank Updegrove Photo.*

View of a team moving a flatcar at winterquarters of RBB&B Circus in 1925. *Frank Updegrove Photo.*

Winterquarters of Sparks Circus at Macon, Georgia, in 1930. Baggage stock enjoying the sun. Note the two horses standing together at left. Long-string drivers often commented that horses that worked together all season would stay together when pastured. In some instances, even a group of six or eight horses might congregate in a pasture—stick together as they did all season. *Jim McRoberts Collection.*

Sparks Circus winterquarters in 1925 at Macon, Georgia, in the spring of the year. The baggage stock, harnessed, is being exercised to harden them up a bit. *Tracy Mathewson Photo.*

In the spring of the year prior to 1919 when Ringling Bros. maintained its winterquarters in Baraboo, Wisconsin, the street resounded to the rumble of heavy wagons as the draft stock was exercised and hardened up. This fine-looking team of Percherons is working out on Walnut Street. *Author's Collection.*

Ringling Bros. Circus winterquarters on Water Street in Baraboo, Wisconsin. The large building on the right was the stable for the draft stock posing in the street in 1910. *Author's Collection.*

About two miles away from winterquarters on Lynn Street near the southwest edge of town, the Ringlings maintained this enormous barn to stable some of their draft stock. It was a three-story building with ramps leading to the upper floors. the Percherons are shown here enjoying the warm sun during a Wisconsin winter. *Circus World Museum, Baraboo, Wisconsin.*

The patches of snow indicate wintertime at the Peru, Indiana, quarters of a number of circuses, all owned by the Ringling banner. This early 1930 photo shows the baggage stock at ease, free to exercise or loaf in the large pasture. *M.D. McCarter Collection.*

Hundreds of grade Percherons were kept at the Peru, Indiana, circus farm for the winter. In the early 1930s, baggage stock of several big railraod circuses were kept here. Good timothy hay and oats were plentiful, and the crisp winter weather was good for the horses. *M.D. McCarter Collection.*

The manes that were roached during the summer season are growing out, as can be seen as the draft stock soak up the winter sunshine at Peru, Indiana, circus winterquarters in the early 1930s. *M.D. McCarter Collection.*

The Bridgeport, Connecticut, winterquarters of Ringling Bros. and Barnum & Bailey Combined Shows included a barn for the draft stock. Frank Updegrove, a Ringling long-string driver, took this photo in the spring of 1927. *Dick & Peg Hemphill Collection.*

Frank Updegrove, a Ringling driver, took this photo of the draft horse barn in spring 1927. Note that clusters of pails are suspended over the horses to keep them from underfoot. The harness and collars are neatly hung at each stall. *Dick & Peg Hemphill Collection.*

CHAPTER 11

The Last Years

Nineteen hundred thirty-eight was the last season *Ringling Bros. and Barnum & Bailey* used draft stock for all the work. *Cole Bros. Circus* followed suit a few years later. Their last year with the Percherons was 1940. This, then, was the end of the line for one of the intrinsic trademarks of the circus, particularly in the preceding thirty years when motor vehicles were pushing horses off the city streets and farms.

To a small degree, the draft horses held on, however. Some teams were used for unloading the trains for a few more years. Other circuses kept a six-up of greys for promotion work. *Ringling Show* kept some teams for specs in their huge tents and, on this show in the mid-1940s, four Clydesdales appeared on a circus for the first time.

As late as 1980, circus owner D.R. Miller said he would love to have a six-horse hitch of Percherons for his *Carson-Barnes Circus.* "I can get all the horses I want," he said, "but where can I find a good reliable horseman today that wants to travel with a circus and can drive six-up." Mr. Miller understands the enormous advertising value of a six-horse team. It would, indeed, attract attention, as is shown at the Circus World Museum in Baraboo, Wisconsin. Here the dapple grey Percherons load wagons on railroad cars and also pull street parade wagons around the property. The noble Percheron is here reduced to being an animated historic display.

Cole Bros. train team in 1949 in Cincinnati, Ohio. This team had to scratch to get the wagons moving. *Harold Gorsuch Photo.*

The dapple greys straddle the rails as they move over the flats on Cole Bros. Circus. All the wheels were hard rubber-tired, which added to the lug for the horses. 1942. *Harold Gorsuch Photo.*

Pull-away team at work on the slick pavement in Hamilton, Ohio, 1942, as Cole Bros. unloaded. *Harold Gorsuch Photo.*

In 1941, Cole Bros. had only four train teams. Dutch Warner, long-string driver (shown here) stayed with the show to care for the horses. *Harold Gorsuch Photo*.

When Cole Bros. Circus unloaded early one foggy morning in Madison, Wisconsin, in 1945, the pullover team really had to dig in to get a wagon moving. *Author's Photo*.

Taking it nice and easy. This Cole Bros. pullover team rolls the wagon toward the runs. 1949 in Cincinnati, Ohio. *Harold Gorsuch Photo*.

This team of Percherons did promotional duty on circus day. They hauled the steam calliope through the downtown district to attract attention. Cole Bros. Circus in Racine, Wisconsin, 1947. *Author's Photo*.

The Ringlings used Percherons to unload their train in 1946. The dual pneumatic tires added materially to the drag on the wagon for the horses at West Allis, Wisconsin. *Author's Photo.*

On Ringling Bros. and Barnum & Bailey Circus in 1943, the Percherons became part of the show. Here they are seen pulling a bandwagon around the hippodrome track in the "spec" that resembled the old-fashioned street parade. *Author's Photo.*

In 1947, the Ringling Circus had as a major spec production "Wedding of Cinderella." In it, the old street parade Bell Wagon was used, drawn by six splendid Percherons. *Author's Photo.*

Probably the first and only time that Clydesdales were ever used on a circus. The Ringling spec used these four for a few years. This photo was taken in 1945 in West Allis, Wisconsin. *Author's Photo.*

In 1950, the Al G. Kelly-Miller Bros. Circus carried six Percherons for downtown promotion work. Here the team is heading across the lot to pick up its wagon. *Harold Gorsuch Photo.*

On the way downtown, the Kelly-Miller team swing wide around a corner so that the wagon won't go over the curb. The harness that these horses are wearing is new style with lots of brass spots and Scotch collars—very unlike the harness of the baggage stock days. 1953. *Author's Photo.*

The hands of Frank Wiseman, who drove the Kelly-Miller six. He was an old-time long-string driver. In the old days, Frank would never have worn gloves. 1953. *Author's Photo.*

The Kelly-Miller Circus carried their six Percherons in this trailer, a far cry from the seventy-two-foot long stockcars of the big railroad shows. 1950. *Harold Gorsuch Photo.*

The sorrel Belgians on the Dailey Show in 1950 were used for downtown advertising to let people know "Today Is Circus Day." *Jim McRoberts Collection.*

In 1950, Dailey Bros. Circus had one 4-up of heavy strawberry roan Belgians that were used, among other chores, to pull the stake driver around the lot, as seen here in Watertown, Wisconsin. *Author's Photo.*

The Dailey Bros. drafters are shown here late in the afternoon in Watertown, Wisconsin, tied to the pole truck in 1950. The harness is a heavy showy type, not at all like the harness used by the baggage stock in their heyday. *Author's Photo.*

So proud was Dailey Bros. Circus owner Ben Davenport of his draft horses that he had a special poster to advertise them. 1950. *John Hurdle Collection.*

Tony Diano, who owned his own circus, had a fine hitch of six Belgians on his show. The hame housings that he used were reminscent of the old parade days. This photo was taken July 11, 1953 in Oconomowoc, Wisconsin. *Author's Photo.*

The daily crowds never tire of watching the great Percherons work. *Circus World Museum, Baraboo, Wisconsin.*

The Circus World Museum in Baraboo, Wisconsin, maintains an excellent team of Percherons. Daily they are hitched to historic circus wagons from the museum's collection. These magnificent animals, the dapple grey Percherons that served the circuses so well, have been reduced to an animated museum display. *Author's Photo.*

Dapple grey Percherons and the circus seem synonymous in the minds of the general public. This breed is flashy, nimble-footed, easy going, and hard pulling. Photo taken at the Circus World Museum. *Author's Photo*.

CHAPTER 12

The Schlitz Circus Parade

It was a bright sunny day in Milwaukee, the Fourth of July 1963. Down the street came the greatest display of circus street parade wagons ever assembled into one grand march. Ray Bast, President of the Percheron Horse Association of America driving his four blacks, led the spectacle.

What glorious wagons they were. What fascinating stories they could tell if they could only talk. Having paraded in large towns and small all across America, many of them fifty, sixty, and some seventy years ago and more, these great vehicles were again doing what they were designed to do—show off and attract attention. This they did. There was the Lion and Mirror Bandwagon from the *Adam Forepaugh Shows* of the 1880s; the three fairy tale floats, *Cinderella*, *Mother Goose*, and *Old Woman in the Shoe* from the *Barnum & Bailey Circus* of the late 1880s. *Pawnee Bill's Wild West Show* was represented in his big bandwagon from 1903. Smaller shows, such as *F.J. Taylor Circus* and *Howe's Great London* were represented. *Gollmar Bros. Circus* Mirror bandwagon; tableaux from *Sparks Circus*; *Golden Bros. Circus* were on the street. Cages and dens from *Hagenbeck-Wallace Circus* and *Sells-Floto Circus* rolled by. The 22-foot-long Swan Bandwagon from the *Forepaugh-Sells Bros. Circus* was in the pageant, as was *Ringling Bros.* Great Britain Bandwagon. There was a music wagon from the *101 Ranch Real Wild West Show*, and the massive Asia wagon from *Christy Bros. Circus.* The whole contingent was followed by *Cole Bros. Circus* steam calliope.

While the event grew annually, as wagons and other displays were added, for an eleven-year span there was one major difference between these Milwaukee circus parades and those staged by the travelling shows of years ago—all of the horses were purebred, not grades. There was one other noticeable difference; in addition to Percherons, there were Belgians, Clydesdales, and in one year's parade a hitch of Shires.

This horse-drawn pageant did indeed indicate that even though the horse-drawn era was long gone, people still had a fascination and love for the horse. Hundreds of thousands thronged the streets of Milwaukee to see this great circus parade every year, and many millions watched on local and national television.

How did this re-created street march come about? One hundred and twenty-five miles northwest of Milwaukee is the city of Baraboo, the hometown of the *Ringling Brothers* and winter quarters for their circus from 1884 to 1918. Here is located the Circus World Museum, a historic and educational museum of circuses of the world. The Museum began collecting historic parade wagons.

The next step was to find a sponsor for reviving the old-fashioned circus street parade. Enter into the picture Mr. Ben Barkin, whose public relations firm had the *Jos. Schlitz Brewery* as one of their accounts. Here at last, after fourteen polite rejections from unimaginative executives of Wisconsin's top-drawer corporations, was a man with a fertile mind. As the old-time street parades were explained and illustrated with historic photographs, the eyes told everything. For the first time there was sparkle, castle-building—a parade for everyone—wholesome family fun, refreshing.

The next step was a visit with Mr. Robert Uihlein, President of *Schlitz*. A decision to sponsor the Museum's historic parade came after twenty minutes of conversation. The rest of the meeting was spent talking about horses.

The event grew each year in size and scope until the last few years the Parade had an estimated 750 horses—over half of them drafters.

As many as sixty-two multiple hitches of draft horses, some ponies, a few lightweight horse hitches, and a couple of mule hitches made up the parade. There were teams from all over the Midwest, primarily, and a few from Ohio, Pennsylvania, New York, Texas, Idaho, and Canada.

Some of the best linesmen in the country were involved. Horses that had won Grand Championships and blue ribbons in major fairs were represented by the dozens.

Listed here are the draft horse teams, mule teams, and the lightweight teams that participated in 1973, the last *Schlitz Circus Street Parade*:

Horseman	Address	Team	Wagon
Adams, Claude	Lamar, Missouri	6 Mules	#201 Stringer Wagon
Allen, Joe	Cozad, Nebraska	6 Belgians	#28 Hippo Den
Barney, Leland	Rigby, Idaho	8 Shires	#72 America Calliope
Bast, Ray	Richfield, Wisconsin	4 Black Percherons	Introduction Wagon
		1 Black Percheron	#219 British Flag Wagon
Bausback, Max	Waldron, Indiana	4 Buckskins	#22 Norris & Rowe
Brass, Archie	Sheboygan, Wisconsin	4 Belgians	#200 40-Horse Announcement
Brass, El Roy	Elkhart Lake, Wisconsin	4 Belgians	#207 Washington Float
		1 Belgian	Cart (Janet Brass)
Brooks, Grayson	Sparta, Wisconsin	4 Clydesdales	#208 Statue of Liberty Float
Callahan, Ed	Ellendale, Minnesota	4 Appaloosas	Concord Coach
Callahan, Phil	Albert Lea, Minnesota	4 Appaloosas	Star Tableau
Chipman, G.E.	Perry, Missouri	6 Mules	#1 Covered Wagon
Circus World Museum	Baraboo, Wisconsin	6 Percherons	#41 France Bandwagon
Clark, Harold	Howell, Michigan	8 Belgians	#1 Lion & Mirror Bandwagon
Coddington, Ralph	Indianapolis, Indiana	6 Black Percherons	#25 *Hagenbeck-Wallace* Cage
Coughlin, Ervin	Watertown, Wisconsin	6 Clydesdales	#24 *Hagenbeck-Wallace* Cage
Eschrich, Robert	Glendale, Wisconsin	4 Black Percherons	#86 Lady & Lion Tableau
Farmer, William	Eaton, Ohio	6 Black Percherons	Our Country Float
Friend, Mrs. John	Hartland, Wisconsin	2 Hackneys	Lead Carriage
Gingrich, Rollin	Parnell, Iowa	6 Belgians	#89 Beauty Tableau
Groves, Jim	Pecatonica, Illinois	3 Clydesdales	#61 *Barnum & Bailey* Cage
Griffith, Herchel	Malcom, Iowa	6 Belgians	#71 Asia Tableau

Horseman	Address	Team	Wagon
Hexom, Arnold	Waverly, Iowa	6 Grey Percherons	#26 *Gollmar* Mirror Bandwagon
Jentes, Lloyd	Wooster, Ohio	6 Grey Percherons	#44 Lion & Tiger Tableau
Keirn, Walter	South Whitley, Indiana	6 Belgians	#55 Band Organ
Kent, Ralph	Embro, Ontario	6 Coach Horses	Temple Tableau
Koester, Ken	Scales Mount, Illinois	4 Spotted Lightweights	#29 *Sells-Floto* Leopard Den
Krueger, Harold	Sparta, Wisconsin	2 Mules	Circus World Museum Cart
Kruger, James	Aurora, Iowa	6 Black Percherons	Gladiator Tableau
Lee, Clifford	Menomonie, Wisconsin	8 Black Percherons	#62 Columbia Bandwagon
Lindsay, Charles	Greencastle, Pennsylvania	4 Palominos	Italian Wagon
McGrew, Miles	Walnut Grove, Illinois	8 Belgians	#100 Great Britain Bandwagon
McMain, Harold	Delmar, Iowa	6 Belgians	#19 *Sells-Floto* Cage
Minor, Sam	Ely, Iowa	4 Grey Percherons	#83 *Barnum & Bailey* Cage
Pierce, Orval	Oakland, Iowa	8 Belgians	#11 Charging Tiger
		1 Belgian	Cart (Dorothy Campbell)
Powers, Mrs. Ed	McGraw, New York	6 Grey Percherons	Twin Lions Tableau
Prochnow, Earl	Athens, Wisconsin	4 Belgians	#81 *Howe's* Cage
Quincy Shrine Club	Quincy, Illinois	6 Belgians	#31 Kangaroo Tableau
Riemer, Ronnie	Chilton, Wisconsin	4 Belgians	#206 Betsy Ross Float
Ropp, Carl	Geneseo, Illinois	12 Belgians	#87 Swan Bandwagon
		4 Palominos	Royal Mail Coach
Rossler, Frank	Menomonie, Wisconsin	6 Belgians	#84 Sea Shell Tableau
		1 Belgian	Cart (Mabel Rossler)
Ruby, Roland	Brookfield, Wisconsin	6 Belgians	#52 Dragon & Mirror Tableau
Schneckloth, Don	Davenport, Iowa	8 Belgians	#75 Fairy Tale Tableau
Shira, Dean	Fredericktown, Ohio	6 Black Percherons	#98 Orchestmelochor
Sparrow, Dick	Zearing, Iowa	40 Belgians	*Schlitz* Bandwagon
		1 Belgian	Cart (Victorine Pierce)
Stichert, Willis	Chili, Wisconsin	3 Belgians	#116 Ken Maynard Air Calliope
Stoeklen, Lloyd	Menomonie, Wisconsin	4 Black Percherons	#33 Sea Serpent Tableau
Struck, Erich	Weyauwega, Wisconsin	6 Clydesdales	#85 Picture Cage
Tribbling, Donald	Markham, Ontario	6 Black Percherons	Golden Age of Chivalry
Westbrook, William	Marengo, Ohio	8 Grey Percherons	#80 *Pawnee Bill* Bandwagon
Woodbury, Keith	Ridgeville, Indiana	4 Belgians	#82 *Howes'* Cage
		2 Tandem Belgians	#20 *Hall Farm* Cage
Wuis, Weldon	Allegan, Michigan	3 Belgians	#88 Whiskers Cage

In the 1973 Parade there were 158 Belgians, 87 Percherons, 19 Clydesdales, 8 Shires, 14 Mules, and 28 lightweight drafters. In addition to the draft horse teams, there were 13 four- and six-up pony teams in the parade.

The fascinating aspect of the big event was that it became an unofficial convention for all draft horsemen. There were as many, or more, horsemen who did not have teams in the parade, but were at the pre-parade showgrounds buying, selling, or trading horses, bragging about ribbons won, complaining about blind judges when ribbons were lost, and most of all, telling stories that were heartily laughed at, and some stories that were not believed.

Much of the friendly yarning was "outuv" stories. "That filly is outuv that Dolly mare who is outuv the champion brood mare at Ohio in '63 who was outuv"—and on and on. All had a great time sitting on bales of hay surrounded by beautiful drafters, well-cared for harness, and wonderful friends.

All the drivers and their horses put on an impeccable performance. Never once in all the years of parading was there even the slightest kind of an accident—the drivers, brakemen, and out-riders were professional—all of them.

On the Fourth of July 1973, the *Great Schlitz Circus Parade* passed into history. This event is covered here because of the significance of the unique, historic, beautiful, and massive circus wagons. This will please all who are interested in the circus and, of course, those interested in draft horses will enjoy this material, too. This book is a "tribute to the Percheron." However, I feel sure that all Percheron breeders happily shared the pleasures of the Milwaukee Parade with their friends that owned Clydesdales and Belgians.

It all began in Baraboo, Wisconsin, where the circus train was loaded. Here the Percherons pull the Columbia Bandwagon up the runs. *Schlitz Brewing Co.*

A young team eases a baggage wagon across the flats. *Schlitz Brewing Co.*

At Milwaukee, the unloading of the twenty-two flatcars is proceeding. A pull-away team is about to take #209 Wagon to the street. Two pullover teams of greys can be seen moving wagons over the flats. Lloyd Jentes, Wooster, Ohio, and his 6-up are waiting the next wagon to take it to the showgrounds. *Schlitz Brewing Co.*

At the showgrounds, nine tents have been erected in which to stable the draft horses. *Schlitz Brewing Co.*

The nine-ton steam calliope comes off the flats. *Schlitz Brewing Co.*

Floyd Jones, Bangor, Wisconsin, busy washing his horses. Here a huge Clydesdale stands patiently, enjoying all the excitement. 1963. *Schlitz Brewing Co.*

Each team owner was required to make a practice run with his assigned wagon to get the feel of the heavy vehicle and to check the brakes. Here Frank Rossler (in cap), Menomonie, Wisconsin, assisted by Ron Reimer, are hitching. *Schlitz Brewing Co.*

Frank Rossler's leaders. *Schlitz Brewing Co.*

Down the street, Rossler's team pulls a massive wagon. *Schlitz Brewing Co.*

Ed Powers of McGraw, New York, brings his Percherons around a corner after finishing his practice run with an ornate wagon that towers seventeen and one-half feet in the air. 1970. *Schlitz Brewing Co.*

A large group of drivers and their teams pose for a publicity photo. All three major draft breeds are well represented in this 1965 photo. *Schlitz Brewing Co.*

Harold Clark, Howell, Michigan, drove in the 1966 parade and many more with his fine Belgian team. His wagon, the "Lion & Mirror," was Ringling Bros. #1 Bandwagon at the turn of the century. *Schlitz Brewing Co.*

Closeup of Harold Clark, a truly great horseman. 1965. *Schlitz Brewing Co.*

Cliff Lee of Menomonie, Wisconsin, drives his six blacks on the Columbia Bandwagon. *Schlitz Brewing Co.*

A view from the driver's seat. Cliff Lee drives his team in 1964 down Kilbourn Avenue in Milwaukee. *Schlitz Brewing Co.*

Cage #25 is being handled nicely in 1967 by Ralph Coddington, Indianapolis, Indiana, and his Percherons. Behind him, Ed Claussen of Gladbrook, Iowa, is moving right along with his six Clydesdales. *Schlitz Brewing Co.*

The big bandwagon was built in 1903 for Pawnee Bill's Wild West Show. Here the eight bay Clydesdales driven by Harold J. Shuert of Syracuse, New York, handle the big load easily in 1965. *Schlitz Brewing Co*.

Herchel Griffith, Malcom, Iowa, hauls the "Asia" tableau down Wisconsin Avenue in Milwaukee in 1971. *Schlitz Brewing Co.*

The six sorrel Belgians blend with the beautiful orange and silver tableau wagon. Rolland Ruby drives his horses in the 1969 parade. *Schlitz Brewing Co.*

In the foreground is Lloyd Stoeklen, Menomonie, Wisconsin, and his blacks, followed by Floyd Conger, Pecatonica, Illinois, and his unicorn hitch of Clydesdales. Just making the corner is the Belgian team of Miles McGrew, Walnut Grove, Illinois. This was the 1967 parade. *Schlitz Brewing Co.*

The six greys are being driven by Victor Cookson, Bowmansville, Ontario, pulling the Mirror wagon from the Gollmar Bros. Circus. Behind the Mirror Wagon are Mrs. Richard Sparrow, Mrs. Dorothy Campbell, Mrs. Frank Rossler, and Mrs. Elroy Brass, driving their Belgian carts in the 1969 parade. *Schlitz Brewing Co.*

Elroy Brass, Elkhart Lake, Wisconsin, starts his four Belgians around a corner pulling a cage full of tigers. The Ringling Circus elephants follow him in this 1964 parade. *Schlitz Brewing Co.*

In 1972, William Westbrook, Marengo, Ohio, drove his eight Percherons (four greys and four blacks) hitched in checkerboard fashion. A real circus touch. *Schlitz Brewing Co.*

The enormous "Great Britain" Bandwagon is drawn by eight Belgians in the 1966 parade. Bert Fevold, Humbolt, Iowa, was driving. Behind him, Bob Jones, Farmer City, Illinois, is driving his six grey Percherons. *Schlitz Brewing Co.*

The hitch of twelve Belgians, driven by Carl Ropp, Geneseo, Illinois, in 1965, was reminiscent of the old-time circus parade long strings. *Schlitz Brewing Co.*

Don Tribbling, Markham, Ontario, drives his six blacks on a 1903 Barnum & Bailey tableau in the 1969 parade. *Schlitz Brewing Co.*

In the first Schlitz Circus Parade in 1963, Parker Taft, Freeport, Illinois, had his eight black Clydesdales hitched to the nine-ton Steam Calliope "America." *Schlitz Brewing Co.*

Dick Sparrow, Zearing, Iowa, brings his forty-horse hitch around a corner. The last time a circus used a forty was in 1904, when Barnum & Bailey hitched up forty matched bay Percherons. *Schlitz Brewing Co.*

TEAM	NAME	VARSITY OR SPARE	AGE	HEIGHT* (in hands)	WEIGHT
LEAD 1	Chappie	V	4	17-1½	2000
2	Duffey	V	6	16-3	2000
3	Rocky	V	6	17-1	2100
4	Pat	V	4	17	1950
9 1	Burt	V	4	16-2	1850
2	Sam	V	5	16-2	1900
3	Ben	V	6	17-1	2150
4	Corky	V	3	16-3	1700
8 1	Roscoe	V	3	16-3	1850
2	Lazy P	V	5	17-1	2100
3	Jeff	V	5	17-1	2050
4	Bingo	V	2	16-2	1800
7 1	Fritz	V	4	16-2	1850
2	Roger	V	4	17	1900
3	Rick	V	4	17-1	1900
4	Gopher	V	5	16-3	1900
6 1	Dooley	V	3	16-3	1800
2	Doc	V	12	17	2000
3	Mark	V	4	17-1	1850
4	Manus	V	4	16-2	1800
5 1	Flash	V	3	16-3	1800
2	Don	V	5	16-3	1950
3	Bob	V	5	16-3	2000
4	Lynn	V	5	16-3	1850
4 1	Ned	V	2	17	1800
2	Tom	V	5	17-1	2200
3	Baldy	V	6	17-1	2200
4	Ray	V	3	17-1	1800
3 1	Mary Ann	V	3	17	1900
2	Rosie	V	4	18	2100
3	Fox	V	4	17-2	2000
4	Baker	V	5	17-1	1900
2 1	Bill	V	7	17	2350
2	Major	V	18	17-2	2100
3	Daisy	V	7	18-1	2200
4	Buck	V	4	17-2	2150
WHEEL 1	Pedro	V	13	17	2200
2	King	V	15	17	2000
3	Chief	V	4	18	2200
4	Lee	V	5	17-3	2200
	Jim	S	2	16-3	1700
	Al	S	4	16-1	1750
	Duke	S	3	16-2	1750
	Pete	S	3	16-2	1700

*NOTE: A hand is 4", thus, a Belgian standing 17-3 hands is 71" tall (17 X 4 = 68 + 3 = 71)

SCHLITZ CIRCUS BANDWAGON

SCHLITZ
40-HORSE HITCH
SCORECARD

The gold and white Schlitz Circus Bandwagon was created specially for the famous Schlitz Forty-Horse Hitch at appearances around the country. Shown in front of the five-ton, twenty-two-foot-long wagon are Dick Sparrow (left), driver of the Forty, and the late Robert A. Uihlein, Jr., chairman and president of the Jos. Schlitz Brewing Company, sponsor of the Forty. The wagon, featuring ornate wood carvings covered with 23-karat gold leaf, made its public debut in the 1973 Fourth of July Schlitz Circus Parade in Milwaukee, Wisconsin. *Schlitz Brewing Co.*

An impromptu and spectacular event took place in 1968 at the lakefront showgrounds during the pre-parade festivities. Dick Sparrow, John Herriott, performance director, and John Luxem, performer, decided to have a Roman standing race. Sparrow provided the two-horse teams, and each of the three men galloped into the ring. Not to be outdone, Lloyd Jentes, a Percheron breeder from Wooster, Ohio, quickly jumped on his wheelers and thundered into the ring at full gallop to the roaring applause of tens of thousands of spectators. He won. *Schlitz Brewing Co.*

Index